Longman

Mainstream
English

J R C Yglesias
& L E Snellgrove

D1806650

STAGE FOUR

An academic course in five graded stages
MASTERY OF ENGLISH
by J R C Yglesias and I M Newnham

Illustrated by Sarah Kensington,
Paul Sample and Designline.

LONGMAN GROUP LIMITED
London
*Associated companies, branches and representatives
throughout the world*

First published 1974
Third impression 1978
ISBN 0 582 23026 8

Printed in Hong Kong by
Sheck Wah Tong Printing Press Ltd

Introduction

Mainstream English is a structured English Language Course graded in six stages. The fifth book reaches the standard and covers the requirements of the CSE examinations. O level examination requirements are covered in the *O level stage* book. This last volume may be taken either as an alternative to *CSE stage 5* or it can follow *CSE stage 5* when O level is taken in the sixth year.

The work is specifically organised with ample variety and grading for use with mixed ability groups. At the same time the series provides opportunities to pursue co-ordinated and integrated studies arising from a particular project.

Language, thought and behaviour are brought together through the medium of certain themes which lead to project work for groups and individuals based on learning situations. But the teacher remains more important than the text; only with his or her guidance can *Mainstream English* achieve its aims. The teacher decides when to develop a project, to pursue an idea, to omit certain sections of work, to skip or to implement according to environmental or personal needs.

It is taken for granted that the teacher will be the most significant audio-visual aid in the class-room. From time to time he or she will teach the whole class and use the blackboard as well as the other visual and audio aids: e.g. film strips, discs and films, which are detailed in this book together with book lists. None the less, the units of work are specifically structured for group and individual work (Organic English). By these means the pupil is helped to turn his competence to good account through interest, involvement and the practice of the necessary language skills. These skills include comprehension, oral work, creative and formal writing (composition), punctuation, vocabulary work, dictionary work, language in use, finding out by reading, etc. There is also scope for role-playing, for classroom drama, for research and for library work. The learning situations have been chosen in an attempt to ensure that language plays an essential part, and there are frequent references to book lists on themes and related subjects.

The theme and project approach is not here regarded as an end in itself. Thus in this series we have tried to be realistic and use this organic and social approach as a springboard to involve the pupil and teacher in English as an essentially practical, stimulating and living language.

For the most part it is assumed that the teacher prefers to deal with pupils' difficulties (spelling, punctuation, grammar, etc.) on an individual or group basis as and when they arise. Nevertheless some work in punctuation, linguistics and grammar is included from time to time as a check for diagnosis and for revision. To sum up:

Mainstream English should train a pupil 'to use the language confidently, appropriately and accurately according to circumstances in which it is used. It should enable him to speak his own mind, to write what he has thought and to have a care for the correctness of written and spoken English. He should be able to understand what he reads and hears, to master ideas and to restate them in his own way. He should have some understanding of the different uses of language, of the language which relates, describes, evokes, persuades and is the instrument of creative imagination.' (*School Examinations Council Bulletin*)

Stage Four covers a year's work and continues with units based on themes with projects. Some of these have a greater 'social' content than in previous stages, e.g. Advertising (Persuaders); Crime and Detection; Countryside, etc. There is increased scope for classroom speaking, miming, and acting situations, and this extended drama work is relevant to the CSE approach to speech and communication.

Another Stage Four feature also relates to next year's CSE work (covered in depth in Stage Five) and provides an opportunity to compile a folder of individual work (a folio of writing) on a limited scale throughout the year.

There is also an increased amount of work on comprehension, composition, and vocabulary. This provides further opportunity to extend language study in a more concentrated form with the inclusion of three separate units where the work set is deliberately divorced from any theme or meaningful context. This exam-like departure will help some to face reality now; others may prefer to delay this confrontation until the CSE year.

Once again, many photographs and other illustrations are designed for visual discussions and awareness as well as documents and decorations. The audio-visual references are included within the relevant units, and Appendix One has further media information and useful addresses. The Book Lists within the units, which range far and wide, must be regarded as a starting point and not a definitive and up-to-date selection. Appendix Two provides a comprehensive cover of Youth Hostelling abroad and relates to Unit 10: *On the move – abroad*.

The encouragement, support and criticism of teachers and pupils again has been invaluable. In particular the creative work of David Adland (author of *Group Approach to Drama, Visual Discussions, etc.*) has been a source of inspiration and enlightenment over many years. A number of passages in this series spring from his general approach to classroom drama.

We hope that *Mainstream English* with its fresh treatment and new approach will be welcomed as a worthy replacement to *Pleasure in English*.

J R C YGLESIAS
L E SNELLGROVE

Note on the second impression

A number of amendments have been made in the interests of accuracy and authenticity. Some new material has been added, especially in Unit 14.

Contents

1 . Night riders and newspapers

Every Saturday night, from suburban homes all over Greater London, hundreds of black-jacketed, teenage motor-cyclists move off in groups towards the M1. Among these groups is one from Kingston-upon-Thames; and one of the seven members of this group is Joe Williams. He is 21 years old and has the distinction of a black jacket made of leather. He works as a builder's labourer for about £15 a week.

When his group arrives at the motorway at about the same time as the others, most of the traffic is going south, towards London. Heading north, Joe's group slowly spreads out along the middle lane, and, one after the other, accelerate away. On some evenings, one or two of them will turn into the third lane and, by accelerating still more and exceeding 100 miles an hour, will 'break the ton'. They thus prove that they are initiates of the teenage cult called the 'Ton Kids'.

Joe's machine is not powerful enough to exceed 85 miles an hour, and the few times that he has done the 'ton', he has been riding on a borrowed machine, soon after dawn, when the roads were almost empty of traffic. After about an hour, the group have covered about 72 miles of the motorway and turn back towards London again. By now, the evening's sport is usually over, and the run back is taken at a steady 50 miles an hour. As they near London they turn off the M1 towards Watford and follow the neon signs to an enormous, glass-fronted transport café, the 'Busy Bee'. Outside there are a few cars, a few coaches, and long rows of shining black and chrome motor-cycles.

It is now eleven o'clock at night. Inside, a long queue of 'Ton Kids' waits for tea and egg and chips, and about 50 are already sitting down talking about motor-cycles. Standing out from this crowd – except for the odd coach party – are a few moderately dressed tourists, who have come along after closing time in the pubs to see what 'coffee-bar cowboys' look like in the flesh. Openly ignored, the tourists are bitterly resented in private conversation. They have come to the 'Busy Bee' with wild stories of teenage recklessness, and some have been advised not to visit it for fear that the 'cowboys' will beat them up.

They watch, with both impatience and trepidation, either for a fight or a display of dangerous skill like the 'roundabout game'. This is allegedly played by putting a record on the juke box, rushing out to a motor-cycle, starting it, roaring off round a nearby roundabout, and returning to one's original position before the record ends. This requires an average speed of more than eighty miles an hour, and it is easier to find people who have friends who have seen it than to find actual witnesses.

All the 'Ton Kids' who were interviewed in the 'Busy Bee' on a recent Saturday night believed that the 'roundabout game' was an impossible one. Although it might have been attempted once or twice, they said, most of the stories about it were nothing but an example of the hostile campaign which is being conducted against teenagers on motor-cycles. The teenagers there were extremely worried by the campaign. They thought it was removing what little tolerance the public ever had for them, and after some discussion Joe Williams was appointed to express their point of view.

'Public opinion is really turning against us,' he

said. 'People in cars, even old blokes on motor-bikes, shake their fists at us as we go past. The police try to pull us in for the smallest things. I don't know what they're trying to prove when they do that, but their attitude doesn't help anybody. When people see a teenager on a motor-bike, they think he must be mad. They'll believe anything about us, so long as it's bad enough. A kid was killed the other day. He was going down a steep hill with two hairpin bends in it, and he slipped and went underneath a lorry coming up. A witness said he was doing the "ton" down the hill, but it's just impossible. You can't get as far down as he did going faster than 35. But if you say the witness was lying you won't get anywhere, because nobody will take any notice.

'The public doesn't seem to realize that it takes skill to ride a bike and that we've been practising for years. The real curses aren't us. They're the car drivers. The other day, I was waiting at some traffic lights next to a vicar. When the lights changed, he swung his car right out in front of me, and he would have had me on the ground if I hadn't been watching

it. He probably talks about teenage hooligans in his sermons, but he's the sort who ought to be banned. The only thing you can do is to keep away from cars as much as possible.

'Only about 10 per cent of kids who ride bikes are these "coffee-bar cowboys", but they're the ones who talk all the time and get us all a bad name. Most of the things they talk about they never do anyway. Most of them don't even have bikes which can do the "ton".

'I only know one kid who doesn't wear a crash helmet. He says it's chicken. He takes off from here so fast that his front wheel doesn't touch the ground till he's on the road. Everybody here thinks he's stupid. He'll fracture his skull soon, and we all know it. Not that I haven't done the "ton". I haven't done it on the motorway either; that's too boring. I've been in one or two burn-ups as well. That's when you're going along and a kid overtakes you. Then you overtake him, then he overtakes you again, and so on. I don't do that now; you only have to come off once to stop yourself doing it again.

'I live for motor-bikes. I don't like my work. I do it for the money and spend it all on the bike. I've less than a quid left for the whole of next week. A teenager's life is really boring these days and motor-bikes have real kicks. The Government ought to do something for teenagers. Youth Clubs are no good. Why do they think I'm interested in carpentry and sing-songs?

'So I come here all the time I can. You get a thrill out of going fast and it's healthy being in the open air like that. It makes you feel good to get dressed up, too, in the black jacket and the boots and the crash helmet with badges all over it. I want a bigger bike now. When you've got a motor-bike you're never satisfied with it; those things really grip you. I don't care what the papers say or what the public thinks, I want a bigger bike and I'm going to get one. It'll set me back about £600 – nearly a year's wages.

'I suppose we'll all grow out of it and settle down one day. I want to start my own business eventually, but I'm not ready for it yet. You've got to have fun while you're young.'

The fact remained, he admitted, that too many teenagers do have serious accidents on motor-cycles, but he thought he had the solution. Nobody should be allowed to have a big machine until they are experienced with a small one, like him. That would stop the young kids, who are the ones, he claims, who have the bad accidents from trying to control a powerful machine they didn't understand.

After a final cup of tea he went outside to his machine. He carefully fitted his helmet on to his head, and with the greatest possible display of restraint he slid slowly into the traffic. To show how careful he was, he went so slowly that he tended to wobble.

MARTIN PAGE *The Guardian*

Reading and reasoning

1 What is the most distinct feature of the appearance of these motor-cyclists?
2 What is the main object of their evening's enjoyment?
3 What is normally the main difference between their north-bound and south-bound run on the M1?
4 For what purpose do late evening trippers visit the 'Busy Bee' and why are they disliked by the motor-cyclists?
5 (a) What do the trippers *most* hope to see happen on their late night visits?
  (b) Why are they likely to be disappointed?
  (c) What do the motor-cyclists consider to be the purpose of the publicity given to this alleged display?
6 What evidence does Joe Williams produce to justify his argument that the public are conducting a campaign against young motor-cyclists?
7 (a) Why is Williams particularly critical of the real 'coffee-bar cowboys'?
  (b) What proof does he give that even their stories are exaggerated?
8 Why did Joe choose a different road from the M1 on which to do the 'ton'?
9 What now prevented Joe from taking part in 'burn-ups'?
10 Explain fully, in your own words, all the reasons for Joe's love of motor-cycling.
11 What proof do you find in Joe's comments that, although he loves adventure and a certain amount of risk-taking, he has little sympathy with sheer foolhardiness?
12 Why did Joe depart with such extreme care?

Interpretation and criticism

1 (a) What is a 'cult'?
  (b) What are 'initiates'?
2 What are neon signs?
3 Why does the writer use the words 'moderately dressed' to describe the tourists who visit the 'Busy Bee'?
4 Which word in paragraph 5 suggests that the tourists are not completely at ease in this café?
5 What is implied by the word 'allegedly' in the statement 'This is allegedly played . . .'
6 What is implied by the use of the word 'hostile' to describe the campaign being conducted against youthful motor-cyclists?
7 Why does Joe Williams particularly quote the example of a vicar in his attack on poor car drivers?
8 Without quoting Joe's example of the Youth Club, try to explain why teenagers might be critical of efforts made by the Government to provide facilities for their entertainment.
9 Try to explain clearly the reason for the appeal to many youths of (a) motor-bikes and (b) the dress used for motor-cycling.
10 What evidence is there in Joe's remarks that he realizes that his love of motor-bikes is probably only a youthful enthusiasm?

Comment and discussion

1 Newspaper articles sometimes reveal bias on the part of their writers. Do you feel that this article shows bias for or against the Night Riders or is it reasonably impartial? Justify your conclusion.

2 A feature of journalistic writing is often the 'live quote'. Compare the styles of writing before and after Joe Williams gives his views. Give reasons for your answers to the following:
(a) How do they differ?
(b) Does the technique of live quotation here add to the article's readability?
(c) Does it help to present an impartial case or not?

3 Why is extensive use made of the 'quote' in journalism?

4 'This is a piece of good journalism.' Journalistic techniques differ from purely literary techniques. Can you find any points of style or vocabulary in this article which indicate that it was written as a journalistic rather than as a purely literary effort? What must a journalist bear in mind when writing for newspaper readers?

Language study

1 Give words similar in meaning to each of these:
    teenage   trepidation   attitude   banned
    fracture   attempted   display

2 Give words opposite in meaning to each of these:
    ignored   hostile   restraint   resented
    original   healthy   powerful

3 The following words have at least two meanings. Find each of them in the preceding passage. Then use each in a separate sentence to show a second and different meaning.
    moderately   roundabout   kicks   conducted
    tolerance.

The three on the right in the illustration are breaking the law.

Composition and creative writing

1 You are a radio commentator. Make a list of questions to put to Joe William's girl friend at the 'Busy Bee' café. Now set down the answers and then write up the whole interview, adding atmosphere by describing the characters standing about for the benefit of your audience. Your report must not take more than three minutes. Record it on tape if you can and compare results.

2 Look back at the second paragraph in this chapter and explain how *they prove that they are initiates of the teenage cult called the 'Ton Kids'*. Now write down suggestions for initiation ceremonies for each of the following:
    an actress   a mountaineer   an MP
    a footballer   a swimmer

When buying a new motorcycle helmet make sure it bears the British Standards Institution Kitemark.

Reading a diagram

Study the graph below, then write a report on your conclusions under the title: Deadly Motor Cycles.

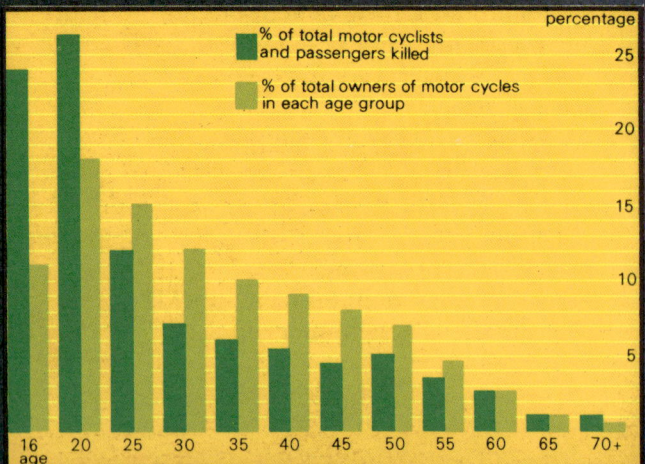

percentage

- ■ % of total motor cyclists and passengers killed
- ■ % of total owners of motor cycles in each age group

25
20
15
10
5

age 16 20 25 30 35 40 45 50 55 60 65 70+

The lorry driver speaks

'When you're away on the road, you're like the captain of a ship, you haven't got people telling you what to do and what not to do.'

'It can be lonely, especially if you're on a long run. You're on your own in the cab and there's nobody to talk to, only when you stop in cafés and meet some of your friends.'

From *The Lorry Driver* by PETER HALLIWELL

Write a couple of sentences describing the feelings of a pillion rider on a motor-bicycle.

Composition and project work

1 Write a short story about the adventures of a long-distance lorry driver on a night run with a valuable cargo.

2 Imagine you have to drive a large lorry a distance of several hundred miles from your school. Work in pairs and sketch a map for a suitable route, bearing in mind narrow roads, congested towns, steep hills, etc. Then prepare short notes giving your reasons for taking the route you have chosen. Either xerox or project your map on a screen and then explain your route to the class. Questions and answers should follow.

Research and discussion

1 Why are Continental lorries often bigger than British ones? Why are some forbidden in Britain?
2 Find out from a dictionary why large lorries are referred to as 'juggernauts'.
3 Consider Bill Naughton's story *Late Night on Watling Street* (Longman Imprint Books) with the accompanying 12in L.P. No. 582 24003.

Reading for pleasure

1 Song of the wagondriver

My first love was the ten-ton truck
They gave me when I started,
And though she played the bitch with me
I grieved when we were parted.

Since then I've had a dozen more,
The wound was quick to heal,
And now it's easier to say
I'm married to my wheel.

I've trunked it north, I've trunked it south,
On wagons good and bad,
But none was ever really like
The first I ever had.

The life is hard, the hours are long,
Sometimes I cease to feel,
But I go on, for it seems to me
I'm married to my wheel.

Often I think of my home and kids,
Out on the road at night,
And think of taking a local job
Provided the money's right.

Two nights a week I see my wife,
And eat a decent meal,
But otherwise, for all my life,
I'm married to my wheel.

B S JOHNSON

2 Jazz fantasia

Drum on your drums, batter on your banjoes,
sob on the long cool winding saxophones.
Go to it, O jazzmen.

Sling your knuckles on the bottom of the happy
tin pans, let your trombones ooze, and go husha-
hush-hush with the slippery sandpaper.

Moan like an autumn wind high in the lonesome
    treetops, moan soft like
you wanted somebody terrible, cry like a racing car
    slipping away from a
motorcycle cop, bang-bang! you jazzmen, bang
    altogether drums, traps,
banjoes, horns, tin cans – make two people fight on
    the top of a stairway
and scratch each other's eyes in a clinch tumbling
    down the stairs.

Can the rough stuff . . . now a Mississippi steamboat
    pushes up the night
river with a hoo-hoo-hoo-oo . . . and the green
    lanterns calling to the high
soft stars . . . a red moon rides on the humps of the
    low river hills . . .
go to it, O jazzmen.

CARL SANDBURG (1878–1967)

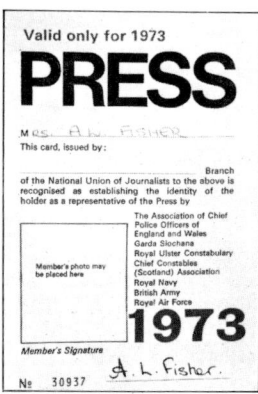

Newspapers and propaganda – for your information

The methods which people use to influence others' actions and beliefs are known as propaganda. For example, you may call the proverb, *It's the early bird that catches the worm* mere propaganda to persuade you to get up early.

At the same time, newspapers may be said to 'slant' the news or give the news a certain emphasis in order to make its readers adopt or believe a particular point of view. This is another kind of propaganda.

Now read on

A Greatly United fully deserved their convincing win over Little Hope in today's top of the league encounter. The score 3–2 hardly reflects the run of the play. United's forwards completely overran the opponents and many brilliant moves which could have doubled the score were frustrated by Little Hope's dreary blocking tactics of cramming the penalty area with as many as six defenders.

B Little Hope belied their name in today's stern encounter. On this form they should go to the top. United wasted attack after attack on over-elaborate moves and only a late error by the brilliantly close-marking Hope defence allowed United to snatch the two points.

Which report gives the less biased account of the game? It is impossible to say. There are almost as many points of view as there are spectators of the game.

Good reporting and reviewing of books, films, and entertainments should be more impartial than the examples above, even if they must reflect the opinions of the readers they cater for.

Give your own report on some recent happening locally or at your school. Work in small groups and compare results to see if you can spot any propaganda.

Alternatively, select one TV or radio programme during the current week. Make notes as you view it yourself. Then work in groups and prepare a review of the programme. Tape the final report and compare group results and differences.

Creative writing

Write two reports on a sports day or swimming gala at another school: the first to emphasize everything good about the occasion, the second to report the occasion in a bad light. You might report on your (imagined) interview with the winner of a particular race. Keep within the bounds of possibility; and do not stoop to lies, or your editor can't print what you write without getting into trouble.

Project work: measure up to it!

1 Work in groups to measure the space given in one or two newspapers to different topics:
    news   sport   fashion   crime
    money matters   sex.
  Work in percentages.
2 Measure the relative amounts of visual material:
    photographs   cartoons   maps   graphs.
3 Measure the relative amounts of advertising space.

Now report which topics in the newspapers you selected received the most space. What topics do you think deserved more space than they received? Justify your answers.

Now consider these two extracts, then answer the discussion questions which follow on the next page.

New Fountain Unveiled

CROWDS GATHERED in West Park on Saturday afternoon to witness the unveiling, by Councillor Sluggett, of the new fountain and paddling pool. This amenity will be much appreciated by the citizens of Little Blissington, particularly by the under sevens who, in spite of pouring rain, did not delay in sampling its delights.

DREAMS

Councillor Sluggett, speaking with some emotion, said that the completion of this enterprise fulfilled one of his dearest dreams and in spite of shortsighted opposition from some quarters would remain for generations of Little Blissingtonians yet unborn a recreational centre of great value and a permanent memorial to a public spirited Council of which he was proud to be chairman.

AFRAID

The centre piece 'Nymphs at Play' by the distinguished modern sculptor Oscar Blemsky, demonstrated that, in matters of art, Little Blissington was not afraid to move with the times. Surprise and resentment might well be felt that several members of the Council had not seen fit to be present at this important ceremony. A severe thunderstorm brought Mr. Sluggett's remarks to a somewhat abrupt close.

'DISGRACEFUL WASTE' SAYS COUNCILLOR

THE NEW FOUNTAIN and statue in West Park, which was unveiled in the presence of a handful of people last Saturday by the Chairman of the Council was described as 'a disgraceful waste of ratepayers' money and a probable danger to to the morals of our young people' by Councillor Matthew Mudd, interviewed in his greenhouse by our special reporter. 'I have opposed the project from the start,' he continued, 'and quite apart from the weather, should not dream of attending the unveiling. Children need discipline, and allowing them to shriek and splash in a public pool is simply encouraging the increase of juvenile crime.' When asked his opinion of the statue which forms the centre piece of the pool, Councillor Mudd repeated: 'Absolutely disgraceful! Art may be all very well in museums but not in an open park for all to see. If we must have art, surely a British sculptor could have been found? I am disgusted.' The *Blissington Herald* now learns that Councillor Mudd has tendered his resignation from the Council in protest. This will be much regretted by all after his forty-seven years of continuous service.

For discussion

1 What do you learn about the size of the crowd from passage 1 and from passage 2 on page 8?
2 Why was Councillor Matthew Mudd interviewed in his greenhouse?
3 What sort of opinion would a reader form about Little Blissington's new 'amenity' from passage 2?
4 What did the reporter responsible for passage 1 feel about the statue? How does this compare with Councillor Matthew Mudd's view?
5 Examine other differences and compare the reporters' intentions in writing their reports.

Follow-up work

Try your hand at similar two-points-of-view interviews over the opening of a new motorway junction in your locality. Or go out and interview 'live' to obtain views on some controversial local topic.

Radio Mainstream

Keeping on the right side

Discuss the following extracts from Radio Mainstream. Point out in what ways this radio station shows bias, and how its reporter Eddy Tooth, has tried to persuade listeners to take sides. Finally show how and where Eddy Tooth has switched loyalties.

October 1

Governor Dixon has categorically denied that he bribed the voters of Minnehaha in yesterday's elections. The whole country supports his fearless stand against such wicked rumours.

October 2

Citizen Kane, interviewed today, gave a confused and totally unsatisfactory account in support of his wild accusations against Governor Dixon.

October 5

Governor Dixon's campaign manager, Dwight R Capone, refused to take part in a face to face argument with Citizen Kane at today's Press conference. New rumours of corruption at the elections are spreading rapidly. No-one is taking them seriously.

October 10

Two voters from Minnehaha have today disclosed on oath that they were offered three weeks free holiday immediately if they would refuse to talk to the Press about the election scandal. Public concern is growing and should be taken seriously.

October 12

Dramatic developments in the election scandal:– Dwight R Capone has resigned his post and detectives have been grilling him about Governor Dixon's involvement in what appears to be a case of bribery. Public opinion is swinging against these public figures.

October 14

Interviewed today Citizen Kane gave a concise and careful account to support his accusations of bribery during the elections at Minnehaha on September 30 last. Governor Dixon refused to comment and when pressed merely mumbled into his beard and went red in the face. Indignation is growing and the whole country supports Citizen Kane's demand for a public enquiry and for the resignation and arrest of Governor Dixon.

October 18

Governor Dixon has at last resigned. Our listeners will also welcome the news that he has today been found guilty of bribery and corruption. Sentence will be passed tomorrow. We have wholeheartedly supported Citizen Kane right from the first and welcome the overthrow of the corrupt Governor and his campaign manager. The whole country supports Citizen Kane in his fearless stand against the corrupt ex-Governor and his henchmen.

Letter writing

Give your school address.
Write a letter of support and sympathy to Governor Dixon.
or
Write a letter of support and congratulation to Citizen Kane.

In either case refer to recent events – but be tactful and choose your words carefully.

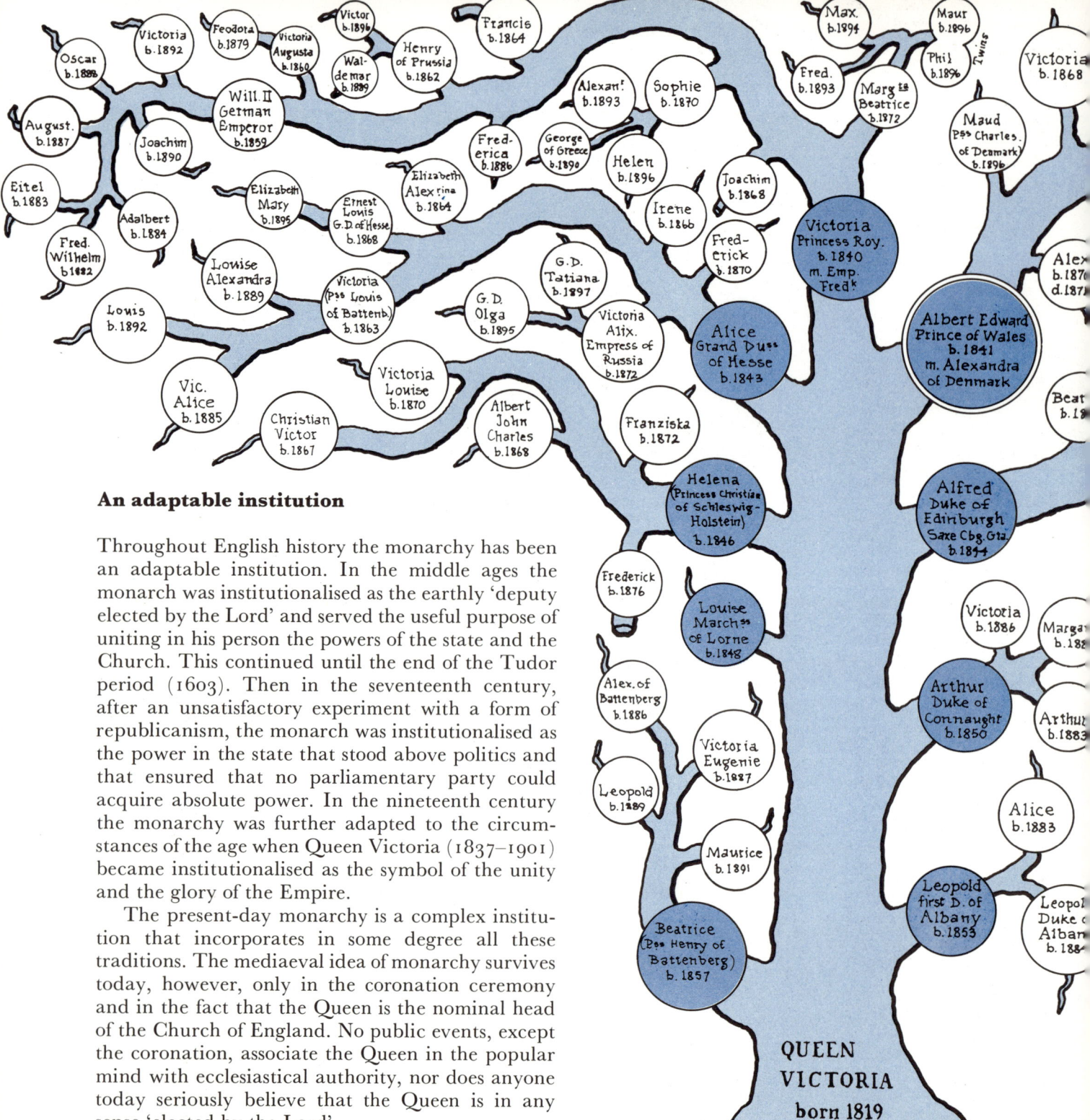

An adaptable institution

Throughout English history the monarchy has been an adaptable institution. In the middle ages the monarch was institutionalised as the earthly 'deputy elected by the Lord' and served the useful purpose of uniting in his person the powers of the state and the Church. This continued until the end of the Tudor period (1603). Then in the seventeenth century, after an unsatisfactory experiment with a form of republicanism, the monarch was institutionalised as the power in the state that stood above politics and that ensured that no parliamentary party could acquire absolute power. In the nineteenth century the monarchy was further adapted to the circumstances of the age when Queen Victoria (1837–1901) became institutionalised as the symbol of the unity and the glory of the Empire.

The present-day monarchy is a complex institution that incorporates in some degree all these traditions. The mediaeval idea of monarchy survives today, however, only in the coronation ceremony and in the fact that the Queen is the nominal head of the Church of England. No public events, except the coronation, associate the Queen in the popular mind with ecclesiastical authority, nor does anyone today seriously believe that the Queen is in any sense 'elected by the Lord'.

STUART HOLROYD The English Imagination

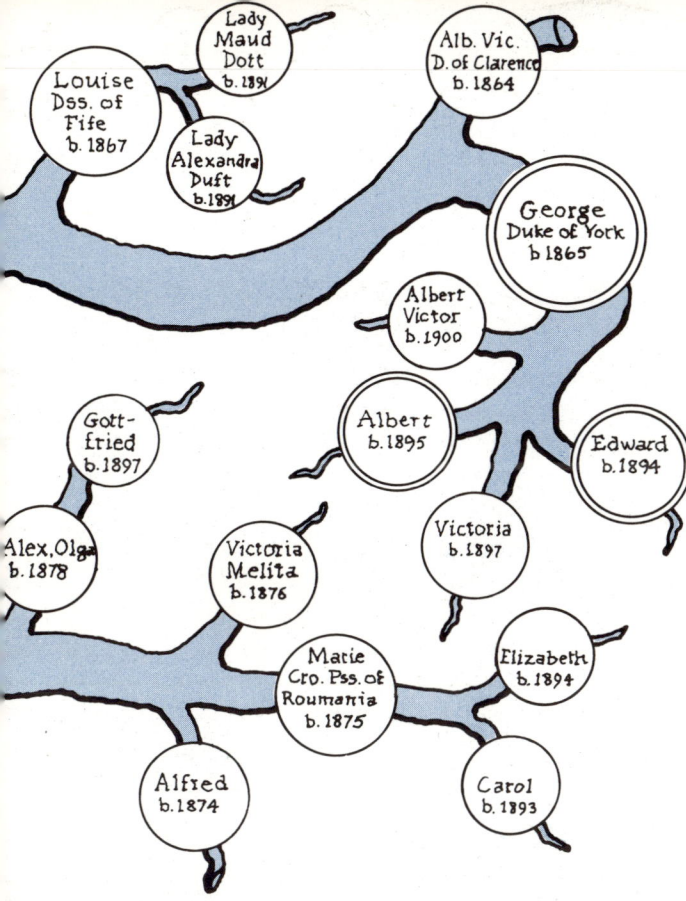

Family tree circles:

Louise Dss. of Fife b. 1867
Lady Maud Dott b. 1891
Lady Alexandra Duft b. 1891
Alb. Vic. D. of Clarence b. 1864
George Duke of York b. 1865
Albert Victor b. 1900
Gott-fried b. 1897
Albert b. 1895
Edward b. 1894
Alex, Olga b. 1878
Victoria Melita b. 1876
Victoria b. 1897
Matie Cro. Pss. of Roumania b. 1875
Elizabeth b. 1894
Alfred b. 1874
Carol b. 1893

This family tree shows the descendants of Queen Victoria up to 1900. Can you show this information in another way?

Try to make your own family tree beginning with a great-grandparent. You may be able to find photographs or drawings.

For discussion

It is now time that the monarchy adapted itself to the changing social circumstances of the second half of the twentieth century. By the time the present heir to the throne is crowned, the life of a monarch will be very different. For example, . . .

By way of contrast

For some time past the King and Queen of Denmark could be seen on their bicycles on their way to the shops in Copenhagen. Once a week they used to eat out at a local restaurant so that their cook could have the day off.

Composition

The advantages and disadvantages of being the child of royal parents.

Headline History

GRAVE CHARGES IN MAYFAIR
    BATHROOM CASE,
ROMAN REMAINS FOR MIDDLE WEST,
GOLFING BISHOP CALLS FOR PRAYERS,
HOW MURDERED BRIDE WAS DRESSED,

BOXER INSURES HIS JOIE-DE-VIVRE,
DUCHESS DENIES THAT VAMPS ARE VAIN,
DO WOMEN MAKE GOOD WIVES?
GIANT AIRSHIP OVER SPAIN,

SOPRANO SINGS FOR FORTY HOURS,
COCKTAIL BAR ON MOORING MAST,
'NOISE, MORE NOISE!' POET'S LAST
    WORDS,
COMPULSORY WIRELESS BILL IS PASSED,

ALLEGED LAST TRUMP BLOWN
    YESTERDAY,
TRAFFIC DROWNS CALL TO QUICK
    AND DEAD,
CUP TIE CROWD SEES HEAVENS OPE,
'NOT END OF WORLD', SAYS WELL-
    KNOWN RED.

WILLIAM PLOMER (1903–1973)

Try your hand at a similar sort of poem.

2. Persuaders

The good old days?

What did we do with our evenings before the age of television? How did we manage to live without detergents, frozen food, plastic buckets, shirts which don't need ironing, materials which won't crease in the wrong places and which keep creases in the right places, socks which needn't be darned, furs which look like furs but are not, laminated surfaces, scooters, spin driers?

Were we really happy without stereophonic sound, Cinemascope, Cinerama, bottled suntan, machines which sell nylon stockings, cola and whisky, ball-point pens, powdered tea, instant coffee, transistor radio sets, electric clothes-brushes, electric shoe polishers, electric tooth-brushes, tranquillizers?

It is sometimes difficult to believe that these make up just part of the endless list of consumer goods which didn't exist in their present form until after 1945.

ROBERT MILLAR

Words at work

Explain the meaning of the following (use a dictionary if necessary):

    detergent   plastic laminated scooter nylon
    instant coffee tranquillizers drip-dry
    transistor

The good old days?

Suggest what people used instead of each of the following before 1945:

    transistor radios detergents ball-point pens
    instant coffee   tights   spin driers
    drip-dry shirts plastic buckets tranquillizers

Is there more in it than meets the eye?

Look at the products in the above photograph.
Discuss to what extent wrapping and packaging
influences the buyer? Consider the packaging of
other products, such as shoe laces. Is the wrapping
worth the extra cost?

Why do they choose?

Fashions in cosmetics change so often that no particular line can ever dominate. The psychologists say that change has a considerable emotional appeal to women; cosmetics prove the point up to the hilt. I failed to find even one woman who was logical about her choice. I would have thought that many would at least choose a range from the same firm.

But no. An Edinburgh woman used Johnson's Baby Powder (one of the cheapest), Yardley's face cream and Elizabeth Arden's lipstick (one of the dearest). A former nurse bought Boots No 7 (inexpensive), Elizabeth Arden (expensive) and Max Factor (in the middle price range). The wife of a civil servant preferred Nivea face-cream, Coty powder, Revlon lipstick. Sometimes she used Charles of the Ritz cream. There was no brand which dominated any aspect of the range . . .

And, despite the fact that cosmetics are related to personal appearance and on that count could be said to be important, many women bought a particular brand because of the pack and not what was inside it. A fashion writer was quite honest: 'I like metal containers. I can't stand cosmetics that are packed in plastic ones', she said.

ROBERT MILLAR

Group projects

1 Conduct a survey by means of a questionnaire on what makes women choose a particular:
    face cream   lipstick   face powder
Try to list the influences which led to her choices. You could interview six girls and the questionnaire might have 'influence' headings such as: price – design – quality – wrapping or container – advertisements. And you could allocate five points to the first influence down to one point for the last. It would be possible, then, to work out a percentage for each arising from the group survey. Working in pairs, each pair could interview six people, one asking the questions the other writing down the reply on the question-naire. Both then co-ordinate the results for their group. Later each pair pools their results and a final percentage could be worked out.

2 Write down in one column this list:
    washing powder   shoes   record player   pen   tie   stockings   shampoo
Opposite each write down the brand you would choose. Try to pinpoint the source of the advertisements which may have influenced you. Compare findings.

3 Write down this list in a column:
    razor blade   coffee   tea   beer   washing machine   chocolates   holidays abroad   shaving cream   soap
Now opposite each article, write down the name of any particular brand which you associate with each of the above. Compare your results and work out the percentage preference for soap, tea, and chocolates for the class.

4 Invent a brand name for a helicopter or for a coach hire firm. Add a slogan, then tape or write a 30 second radio commercial for one of them.

Role playing – work in pairs

You have been appointed a saleslady/man for Green's Salad Cream. Work out a sales talk and try it on a shopkeeper. Exchange roles, and if you tape your scripts, compare them afterwards. Do the same for a book of your choice.

Qualities

1 What particular qualities (e.g. price, durability, design, etc.) would you look for in choosing each of the following:
    soap   tea   tights   trousers   shirt   record player   TV   guitar
Work in small groups and compare results.

2 Explain the difference between wool, cotton, and nylon.
Give examples to show the advantages of each for various garments.

Are men and women much the same?

1 Write a similar or contradictory paragraph to Robert Millar's one on fashions in women's cosmetics but dealing with men's fashions – in jackets or trousers or shirts or hair styles or shoes.
2 Do most men and most women slavishly follow fashion in clothes and hair-styles or are women more individual in their tastes?

The poet speaks

The twenty-fifth of December

Pile the windows high
till they almost crack,
heap the monumental
junkpile of Christmas,
forty-nine price tags
and a picture of Santa Claus,
fifty-nine price tags
and a barber-pole-candy-cane,
hark the herald angels
sing all sales final,
peace on earth and mercy
to all cash customers,
O little town of Bethlehem
ONLY TWO SHOPPING DAYS
Noel, Noel,
Scotch pines $2·50
sixty-nine price tags
and a tinsel-coloured sky,
Good King Wenceslas
in the bargain basement –

Merry Christmas
suckers
                    RAYMOND SOUSTER

Topics for discussion

What's Christmas all about anyhow?
To what extent is Mothers' Day commercialized?
To what extent is your kitchen stocked with products advertised on TV?

Advertising and the Marlowes

The Marlowe family relaxed, well satisfied with the new decoration. The new wallpaper gave their small lounge the distinguished look of a Riviera villa.

Julie was tired. 'When you're tired and nervous energy is low, then the germs attack unknown and unnoticed,' she muttered, reaching for a bottle of pills and swallowing several.

'How right you are!' rejoined her mother, moving into the kitchen and filling the kettle. 'We'll have a cup of tea. Millions of people drink this tea daily to relieve fatigue. They can't all be wrong,' she added with a satisfied smile. Mrs Marlowe's smile was her pride. Her shimmering teeth made her the most popular woman in the neighbourhood.

Margaret, Julie's elder sister, returned from the bathroom, wearing a smart party dress. She was meeting Simon in half an hour. She moved over to the mirror, and began applying make-up.

'Margaret is going to lend me that perfume tomorrow,' sighed Julie. 'Isn't it divine? It smells of moonlight, tropical sunsets, blue velvet skies and romance.'

'Borrow it now,' replied Margaret. 'It'll make you feel much better – lift you beyond your own dreary personality,' she added, without malice.

Their father snorted, 'You keep your perfumes,' he said. 'When you're feeling foul, find a Fag,' with which statement he produced a packet of twenty Filter-Tipped Fags, selected one, and lit it. Clouds of blue smoke ascended to the newly-painted ceiling. Mr Marlowe coughed violently, and then settled down.

John Marlowe looked with scorn at his sister's antics before the mirror, then turned to his magazine. 'Dad!' he exclaimed suddenly, 'there's a picture here of Canterbury Cathedral, where we were last year.'

Without checking whether anyone was interested, John began to read the wording underneath the picture. 'Canterbury . . . guardian of all that is best in England, all that makes England healthy . . .' his voice began to rise with annoyance, 'Protectem toothpaste . . . .' he went on, then exclaimed loudly, 'Oh, heck! it's an advert!'

During the burst of laughter that followed, Mr Marlowe turned on the television. The Marlowe family relaxed, watching the advertisements.

Interpretation and discussion

Advertisements are an all too familiar part of everyday life. The purpose of this study unit is not to give the impression that they are a great social evil, but to make you think straight. Are you gullible? How do advertisers exercise their powers of persuasion?

Before you attempt the following exercises, write down from memory as many advertisement slogans, catch phrases or songs as you can.

The new wallpaper gave their small lounge the distinguished look of a Riviera villa.

1 Can this statement be taken literally? What alterations would the Marlowes have to make to their home in order to give it even a vague look of a Riviera villa?
2 Do you consider it desirable that a small suburban house should look like a Riviera villa? Explain your answers.
3 The advertiser is trying to suggest that his wallpaper will give to the purchaser's house a look of *distinction*. Is this necessarily true?
4 He is making a direct appeal to the buyer's feelings. To which actual emotion is this particular appeal made?
5 Do you consider this to be a fair method of advertising? Give your reasons.
6 Collect examples of advertisements which appeal to this same emotion.
7 Suggest reasons why this type of advertisement has increased recently.
8 Is it only advertisements that appeal to the reader in this way? Collect examples from stories, articles from magazines, illustrated papers – even popular songs that appeal to our sense of snobbery.

'Isn't it divine? It smells of moonlight, tropical sunsets, blue velvet skies and romance.'

1 What is the correct meaning of the word *divine*? Can it properly be applied to perfume?
2 Is Julie's statement, quoted above, literally true? What effect is the advertiser trying to create by describing his product in these terms? Answer in a full paragraph.
3 Collect examples of advertisements which suggest that the purchaser will be transported into a romantic dream world. Other similar examples suggest that the user will enjoy immediate success or wealth. Collect a few of these and write a comment on each.
4 Consider advertisements that suggest, for example, that cooking the Director's dinner with a certain brand of fat will bring the husband immediate promotion; or that the use of a certain hand cream or soap will bring worldwide success to an actress. Are such happenings common in life? Would they not have happened anyway? To what sort of people does this approach appeal?
5 Can you give any reasonable explanation why this type of advertisement appears mainly in magazines intended chiefly for women?
6 What is meant by the word *escapism*? It is said that too much escapism is bad for us. Why? Is there any relation between the type of advertisement under discussion and escapism? Football can be described as a form of escapism; so can reading. Is there a difference between escapism and relaxation?
Make two columns: head one *escapism* and the other *relaxation*. In the first, list those forms of activity which you consider escapism and dangerous if practised too much; in the second, list what you consider to be healthy activities.
7 Select six advertisements for cars from any source. Then describe how each tries to persuade you to buy a car.
How many mention the following factors: safety; miles per gallon; after-sales service?

'*When you're tired, and nervous energy is low, then the germs attack.*'

1 Consider the following slogans:

A *wise* young man will prepare for old age.
What would happen to your *children* if illness struck you?
Can you wear that *old* suit much longer?
What can *they* be thinking at the office?
Even your closest friends will avoid telling you about your bad breath; they'll avoid *you*.

Each of the above approaches depends on the reader being afraid of something. Do they succeed by reducing the reader's worries or increasing them?
Collect a variety of advertisements of this type and say what *particular* fear is aroused in each.

2 What is the correct term for a person excessively preoccupied with and worried about his health?

3 Is it undesirable to make money out of people's fears? Give reasons for your answer.

'*Millions of people drink this tea daily to relieve fatigue. They can't all be wrong.*'

1 What is the meaning of the word *gregarious*? Can the above quotation be said to apply to our gregarious instinct? Is Mrs Marlowe's statement that *they can't all be wrong* necessarily true?

2 The suggestion is made that the *majority* of people drink it. Is this misleading?

3 Is it always sensible to believe that the majority opinion is right? Give your reasons, and add an example of when you consider that the majority opinion may be wrong.

4 Now compare these two approaches:

Millions of beautiful women use this face cream.
Last year, we sold 7 461 241 tubes of face cream.

Which approach has the more direct appeal? Which is nearer to truth and reality? Which is more likely to succeed? If you select the first, which *word* does the trick? Do all these types of advertisement appeal to the public by *facts* or by *suggestion*?

Consider the following:

Thousands of wise men have already prepared for their deaths. Are you going to be the one whose widow is pitied by the neighbours?

This is a combination of appeals already discussed. Explain the various emotional levels being attacked.

The perfume bought by millions that gives you distinctive individuality.
The book that appeals to the discriminating few.
Be different! A well dressed man will always wear a Super Shirt.

1 To what instinct is the appeal directed in the above?

2 In what way is each statement contradictory?

3 Suggest the reaction of a thoughtful person to each.

When you're feeling foul, find a Fag.

1 The most successful advertising slogans are usually brief and frequently repeated. Why do you think this is so? Why are they often in verse or song form?

2 Consider a day in the life of a man who works in a London office, travelling and returning by train and tube. List all the places where he will read slogans automatically. Start with the cereal packet at breakfast. What is the stratagem employed by the advertisers with this constant repetition?

'*Protectem Toothpaste,*' he went on, then exclaimed '*Oh, heck, it's an advert!*'

If you look out of the window before leaving for school, and it is raining, you usually think of putting on a raincoat. Most mental connections are sensible. Is the connection of Canterbury Cathedral with toothpaste sensible?

Copy writing

Make up a brand name and supply a slogan for: a guitar, a shampoo, a cake, a kettle, shoes.

For your information

So far we have examined the methods of certain types of advertisements. Most products on the market are of good quality. We must learn both to discriminate and to be attracted only to products we need and can afford. We must neither automatically accept a product as good because it appears on television, nor take up the attitude that advertising is a bad influence.

To keep a balanced enquiry, consider the *importance* of advertising. Look at your local newspaper and Post Office or small shop window. What is the essential difference between the advertisements you see there and those you have already discussed?

You can't help yourself, can you Madam?

Make no mistake about it – the modern supermarket is a scientifically-designed human mousetrap. And you, the customer, are the mouse. If you don't believe that, consider this fact: the average supermarket shopper, even armed with a full shopping list, will buy an extra 40p of goods for every £1 they had originally intended to spend.

Ask for an explanation and they'll say something like, 'Oh, I just happened to see something that caught my fancy.' The truth is they didn't just 'happen' to see that extra item – the supermarket men had planned it that way. The human mice had fallen for the bait.

See how the supermarket man goes about his business which, like any other business, is simply to sell you as many of his goods as possible.

Nothing wrong with that. But there is one great difference between self-service trading and personal salesmanship. If a salesman at the door is handing out a line of patter, you *know* he is trying to sell you something and you know what that something is. You are on your guard.

The supermarket men don't use patter and warm, friendly smiles. More often than not you never even see them. But they are still giving you a hard sell. So how do they go about it? Just what are the tricks of the trade to get those extra pence we had not intended to spend?

The first aim of the supermarket man is to get you into the supermarket, *his* supermarket. And the main ways of doing this are by advertising cut-price bargains and – not so obviously – the careful projection of special 'images'. These images are designed to make you think a particular supermarket group has its own special virtues.

Some supermarkets trade by the use of brash 'special offer' campaigns, some do it with trading stamps. Others foster the 'image' of scrupulous cleanliness or of guaranteed quality without gimmicks. Think of the supermarkets you know and see how they will fall into one or other of these categories.

Once you have swallowed the ground bait and have been tempted inside, the selling really begins. Now each supermarket operator has his own system, worked out as a result of scientific surveys on how human beings – and housewives particularly – think and behave when they are shopping.

But one way or the other, the same general methods are used.

Let's step inside a supermarket, to the pile of wire baskets and trolleys by the door. The trolleys may even have a seat for the youngster. You take a trolley – and already you have fallen into the first trap. Of course the trolley is nice and convenient but it also helps to prevent you realising just how much you are buying. You don't feel the weight that could serve as an early warning that maybe you are spending more than you intended.

You hum a merry little tune to yourself, echoing the music on the loudspeakers – and that is exactly what you are meant to do. For the music along with the carefully-chosen bright colours and gay displays, is there to suggest that shopping is fun. It relaxes you into the shopping mood.

It's a big supermarket and yet, somehow, you feel nice and cosy. The floor pattern could be helping there, since supermarket scientists have found that when the customers feel over-powered by the vastness of their surrounds they tend to 'freeze-up' – and they don't spend. So often a floor pattern is used to create the illusion of compactness, cosiness and friendliness.

All very well, but so far you haven't actually *bought* anything. Don't worry, they are ahead of you on that one, too. For the head-shrinkers who work out supermarket methods have discovered that there's a curious reluctance to make the *first* purchase, to break the ice.

So, very likely, as you go in there will be a prominent display near the door of something you were almost certain to buy, say, bread or tea, or a tempting cut-price offer. That is to get you into the shopping mood and just in case you are using a shopping basket and not a trolley, it's usually something light so that, again, you don't become conscious of the weight too early.

Right, now you're inside the supermarket and they've started you on your shopping. The next ploy is simple enough – it's how to make you buy as much as possible.

What do the supermarket boffins regard as the ideal human mousetrap? It is simply one long straight aisle where you see everything that is on display. You can't get side-tracked or take any short cuts and eventually you arrive at the check-outs where the nice woman with the nice smile takes your money.

This might be ideal but it's not practical. Stores are built as either squares or rectangles and the check-outs are not at the far end of a mythical corridor. In fact, they tend to be right next to the very door you went in.

The problem now is to make you 'wander' through the whole shop, for the supermarket men have one maxim in common: 'If you don't see it, you won't buy it.' They have to make sure that you see it, to make you wander as if by accident all over the store so that you do see – and are tempted by – as many goodies as possible.

And to get you to wander around they use a device known in the trade jargon as 'playing the winners'. The object, again in their own peculiar jargon, is to make you 'shop the store'. To make you do this, the supermarket men divide their goods into three categories which they call 'Demand', 'Semi-

demand' and 'Impulse'. 'Demand' items are things like tea, sugar, butter, bacon, baked beans, toilet paper and detergents which figure high on any usual household shopping list.

The 'Semi-demand' category includes marginal luxuries like a more expensive brand of tea or coffee, canned vegetables, chocolate biscuits, ready-baked cakes, paper napkins and so on. And 'Impulse' goods could be canned asparagus tips, deodorant aerosols, deep-frozen scampi, cake toppings and Chow Mein – all of which might make life a bit more pleasant but without which you could survive.

ALEX VALENTINE

Project and group work

Compare and check some of the findings in this article as against what you find in your nearest supermarket. Do your findings coincide? List points of difference in note form. Then write a factual report called 'Watch it shoppers or you'll spend an extra 40p!' based on your local mouse-trap (supermarket).

The poet speaks

Superman

I drive my car to supermarket,
The way I take is superhigh,
A superlot is where I park it,
And Super Suds are what I buy.

Supersalesmen sell me tonic –
Super-Tone-O, for Relief,
The Planes I ride are supersonic.
In trains, I like the Super Chief.

Supercilious men and women
Call me superficial – me
Who so superbly learned to swim in
Supercolossality.

Superphosphate-fed foods feed me;
Superservice keeps me new.
Who would dare to supersede me,
Super-super-superwho?

JOHN UPDIKE

THIS WEEK'S BARGAIN 19P

Shopper's guide to the super-trap

Here is a typical supermarket scene, showing the floor-to-ceiling bait that traps you into spending more than you intended . . .

Music: to lull the shopper into a euphoric mood in which buying will be a pleasure

Arrows: to guide you along the route the supermarket planners want you to take

Impulse: high-profit 'impulse-buying' goods are placed strategically at the shopper's eye level

Meat: backed by pink lighting to make sure it catches your eye, the meat is placed as far from the entrance as possible. So you have to walk the full length of the store to get this essential item. Then you're led on to the foods that go with it

Eyecatchers: this time for the children. The idea is that they pester Mum and she's too busy to argue. Result: more sales

Trolley: so easy to pile more and more things into it. And you don't feel the cost piling up

Flooring: the pattern is broken up so that the customer feels more cosy – and more like spending

22

Language study: weasel words

1 Read this extract by David Ogilvy from *Confessions of an Advertising Man*, then find evidence from advertisements which prove some of the assertions he makes.

'The two most important words you can use [in advertisements] are *free* and *new*. You can seldom use *free*, but you can always use *new* – if you try hard enough. Other words and phrases that work wonders are: how to, suddenly, now, announcing, introducing, it's here, just arrived, important development, amazing, sensational, remarkable, magic, offer, quick, easy, hurry, last chance, wanted. Headlines can be strengthened by the inclusion of emotional words like: darling, love, fear, proved, friend, baby.'

2 Now read Paul Stevens's view and answer the questions which follow.

An American, Paul Stevens, considers that weasel words (as he calls them) are smuggled into advertisements to make the products seem better than they really are. For example, toothpaste which '*helps* prevent tooth decay'. If the toothpaste really did prevent tooth decay the word helps would be unnecessary. Apparently years ago Ajax claimed to clean 'like a white tornado' – the word *like* Stevens claims is the advertiser's dream because he doesn't have to substantiate anything. Other weasel words are: enriched, worth, fresh, virtually. Equally, who is the mysterious authority for those advertisements trying to sell briefcases, carpets and unusual underwear which say something like '*worth £10, yours for only £6.*'

Find advertisements with some of the above weasel words. Does their use seem to make the product more desirable at first sight?

3 Favourable or unfavourable impressions can be created by selecting words in terms of associations that have grown up through usage. *Well-known*, for example, is reasonably neutral, *famous* is much more favourable, while *notorious* is clearly unfavourable. Now complete the table and add three examples of your own.

Neutral	Favourable	Unfavourable
dog		
		mob
	perfume	
politician		

4 Consider this statement by Leslie Adrian:
'Look at packets and jars. Half full, two-thirds full, false-bottomed, odd-shaped. No weight given. No quantity stated.'

Examine this statement on the evidence you can produce (for and against) from detergent bottles – boxes of confectionery – instant coffee – bath essence – packets of biscuits.

Summary and research

1 Write a summary of the following in not more than thirty words:
    Beneath this slab
    John Brown is stowed
    He watched the ads
    And not the road.

When we consider the extent of modern advertising it is not surprising that poor John Brown was distracted from his driving. It is not easy to ignore the glossy exaggerations and slick repetitions which accompany our reading matter, shopping expeditions, and entertainment.

2 Discuss an advertisement you consider to be:
  (i) unhelpful and misleading;
  (ii) reliable and reasonable.

3 Write your own advertisement for one of the following (adopt any brand name you like or make one up):
sausages   tennis rackets   T-shirts   jeans
leather coats   shampoos   scent

4 Say how and where you would advertise your school play.

5 Write separate notices for the local paper advertising two of the following for sale:
    a puppy   a kitten   a record player   a bicycle

6 Find out the cost of one of the advertisements you wrote.

Creative writing

Write an advertisement for one of these film titles.

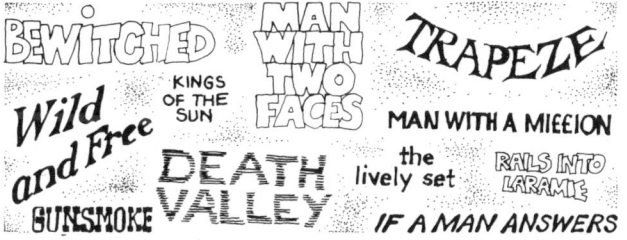

Now design a poster advertising one of these titles.

Visual discussions

Study the advertisement below, then write a few snappy sentences advertising whatever you think connects with this poster. Give your writing a 'selling' slant.

Now tell the story of how this harassed husband was quarrelling with his wife, and failing at his job owing to the domestic strain of housework – until they bought – you decide what they 'invested' in. Try to write persuasively and sell your product to the busy readers!

If you have no time to read ~ read this!

It's just for you

You and your world – Commercial TV

Study this script, and the story board sheet. Then set out your own 30 second script and story board for a TV commercial for any product you like. Use the above structure and formula. Make up your own names for products and people.

Preliminary stills _Suggest blond —_
Attached Miss North who is available.

STORY BOARD SHEET

4 M – Creative Department
Mainstream Agency Ltd.
Harlow Essex
T.V. Commercial Script

Producer _M4 – Ray Denton_

Production Company _Burnt Mill Studios_

Director _Cornford_

Lighting/Cameraman _Graham Portlock_

Music details _None_

Commentator _Roger Watson_

Artists _None_

Medium _T.V._

Client _Supermarket Setup Ltd._

Product _Cutie Chocs_

Job number _9/82666_

Title _Boxes and candies_

Length _30 seconds_

Date _31 March_   Signed _Bert Price Smith_

Special comments

Musical background to be discussed
with clients at next meeting.

vision	sound	vision	sound

1 Display of chocolate boxes

1½ seconds mute

5 DISSOLVE TO Group of attractive girls round box and tasting.

Just look at her and her friends!

VOICES:

Super! What flavour — wish Lionel gave me. Cutie Chocs — I do love that pretty box

2 DISSOLVE TO close up of pretty girl excitedly opening box of CUTIE CHOCS

VOICE OVER:

Miss Allsorts is a modest kind of girl but not when it comes to the contents of these handsome boxes.

6 DISSOLVE TO Box showing CUTIE CHOCS prominently

CHORUS:

Cutie Chocs for me from now on!

3 DISSOLVE TO Cutie box of chocolates Miss Allsorts tasting one of them

You see they contain some of her favourite chocolates. Cutie Chocs.

7 DISSOLVE TO Handsome boy giving Miss Allsorts a box of Cutie chocs, loving expressions etc. girls in back ground

Cutie Chocs are in a class of their own, and thank goodness Jonathan has good taste, too!

4 DISSOLVE TO Cutie Chocs again being tasted, by Miss Allsorts

She's been eating chocolates for some time but these are different!

8

26

The poet speaks

Telling lies to the young is wrong.
Proving to them that lies are true is wrong.
Telling them that God's in his heaven
and all's well with the world is wrong.
The young know what you mean.
   The young are people.
Tell them the difficulties can't be counted,
and let them see not only what will be
but see with clarity these present times.
Say obstacles exist they must encounter,
sorrow happens, hardship happens.
The hell with it. Who never knew
the price of happiness will not be happy.
Forgive no error you recognise,
it will repeat itself, increase,
and afterwards our pupils
will not forgive in us what we forgave.

                    YEVTUSHENKO

For discussion

Can you find examples to argue for or against the above point of view? For example is it wrong to tell the young that Father Christmas exists because this is a lie?

You explain its meaning:

If a man has good corn, or wood, or boards, or pigs to sell, or can make better chairs or knives, crucibles, or church organs than anybody else, you will find a broad, hard-beaten road to his house, though it be in the woods.

          RALPH WALDO EMERSON (1803–1882)

Filmstrips

3 filmstrips in colour: About Shopping; About Care Handling; About Teltag; (from the Consumer Council).

Film

There is a 16 mm sound film in colour (70 mins) which is a cartoon version of *Animal Farm*. Distributed by Columbia Pictures Corporation, 142 Wardour Street, London W1V 4AH.

Selected reading

RUDYARD KIPLING *The village that voted the earth was flat* Macmillan
GEORGE ORWELL *Animal Farm* Penguin. Longman HLS
LEONARD WILLSHER *The pound in your pocket* Cassell
LEONARD DE VRIES *Victorian posters* Murray

For your enjoyment and further research

Research work

Follow up some of the references in these old poster advertisements. For example, *Lillie Langtry* was a very intimate and personal friend of King Edward VII, but who was *Millais* and can you find a reproduction of his first 'Bubbles' picture? And what about *curly-haired Fauntleroys*? Is *tonic wine* alcoholic? Which of these products is available today? Compare costs then and now.

For discussion

What is the particular appeal underlying each of these posters? Does it aim to arouse the senses, or reason or emotions? Or is there a mixture of appeals?

To take you further

Design a poster for any product you like. Then state briefly the aim of the appeal you have used or the mixture (senses, reason, emotion).

Pears' Soap　Pears' Soap

"Two years ago I used your soap, since when
I have used no other."

—*Punch*, April 26th, 1884.

"For years I have used your soap, and
no other."

Lillie Langtry

PEARS' SOAP

SPECIALLY FOR THE COMPLEXION

"MORE BUBBLES" by EDOUARD FRÈRE.
A Companion to "BUBBLES" by SIR JOHN MILLAIS, BART. &c.
Both the Original Paintings in the possession of the Proprietors of

PEARS' SOAP. 'Reg^d Copyright'

DINNER AND SUPPER DAINTIES.
CLEVER RECIPES ARE GIVEN AWAY
WITH EVERY PACKET OF BIRD'S CUSTARD POWDER.

heartily recommend it. Eggs may dis-
e . . . this will not.
"GORDON STABLES, C.M., M.D., R.N."

BIRD'S CUSTARD POWDER

This admirable substitute for
eggs is most enjoyable with
Tinned and Preserved Fruits,
and provides an
endless Variety of
Choice Dishes.

SOLD EVERYWHERE

in 6d. Boxes,

Sufficient for Three
Pints.

1s. Boxes,

For Seven Pints.

A GREAT LUXURY.

PASTRY AND SWEETS,"
GRATIS.

The New and Enlarged Edition of this valuable little work, containing Practical
Hints and Original Recipes for Tasty Dishes for the Dinner and Supper Table, will be
sent, *post-free*, on receipt of address, by ALFRED BIRD and SONS, Birmingham.
N.B.—Grocers can have copies for distribution among their customers on application.

MARIANI WINE

MARIANI WINE Quickly Restores
HEALTH, STRENGTH,
ENERGY & VITALITY.

MARIANI WINE
FORTIFIES, STRENGTHENS,
STIMULATES & REFRESHES
THE BODY & BRAIN.

HASTENS
CONVALESCENCE
especially after
INFLUENZA.

His Holiness
THE POPE

writes that he has
fully appreciated the
beneficent effects of
this Tonic Wine and
has forwarded to Mr.
Mariani as a token of
his gratitude a gold
medal bearing his au-
gust effigy.

MARIANI WINE

is delivered free to all parts of the United Kingdom by WILCOX & CO.,
83, Mortimer Street, London, W., price 4/- per Single Bottle, 22/6 half-
dozen, 45/- dozen, and is sold by Chemists and Stores.

3. Group A folder work

General introduction

This is the first of four *Folder work* units:
A B C D (see also pages 71, 101, 121.) Each section there is a group of studies from which you can choose work for inclusion in your personal folder or wallet. In this way you can build up a folio of your own writing as a result of your selections.

These work studies need not be presented in an elaborate wallet, but a stiff cover and stapling would be appropriate in order to hold together your loose sheets. It is not necessary to cover all the work suggested in all four groups of studies. This first group (A) concentrates on research.

For your information

Read the three extracts below, then carry out the research work which follows:

1 *What makes a good shoe*
The parts of a shoe are shown in the Diagram.

The inside edge of the shoe must be straight enough, and the front must be long, wide and deep enough to allow complete freedom for the toes as far back as the widest part of the toe joints – which should be the widest part of the shoe. There must also be some way to stop the foot sliding forward during walking, otherwise the toes will be cramped into the toe of the shoe. A lace or bar fastening or elastic gusset further up than the widest part of the shoe, together with a snug fitting heel, can keep the foot from slipping forward. An adjustable fastening

also gives a 'tolerance of fit' for growth and for changes in the foot size caused by warmth and cold.

The shoe should also have a strong but resilient shank, preferably of steel, fitted between the inner and the outer sole. This will keep the sides of the shoe from gaping around the instep, and help it flex in the right place – the sole should flex across the widest part, where the toe joints are.

Finally, it must be sufficiently smart and attractive to be acceptable to its wearers.

Teenage girls' shoes,
from *Which?*

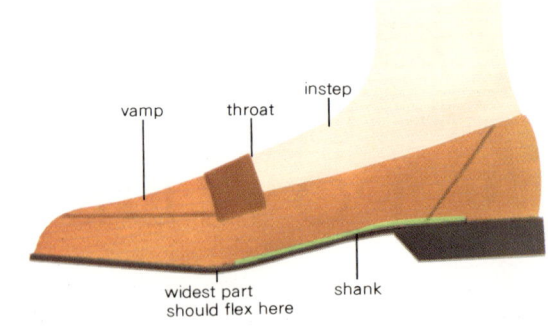

2 *Toe deformities*
At the moment, 88 per cent of all senior schoolgirls have toe deformities, mainly caused by badly fitting shoes. The number of boys with similar troubles is going up as they too become fashion conscious, and move into adult-style shoes at an earlier age.

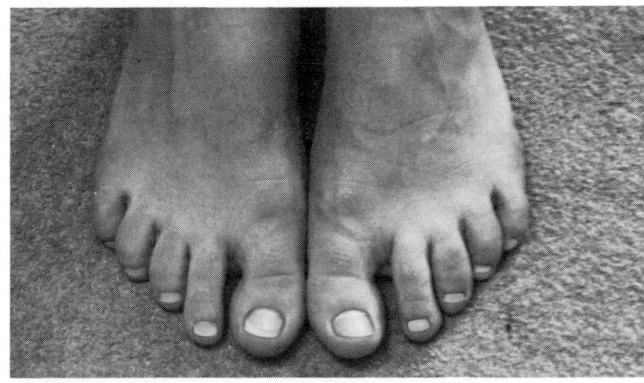

Feet of a thirteen-year-old girl with healthy feet and toes.

Many mothers assume that if the child does not complain of cramped toes, all is well. But children's bones are softer than adults' and more easily pressed into the wrong shape. Pain does not start until matters are desperate, long after the damage is done.

Thousands of these children will be crippled by middle-age, some will need operations to correct bunions and hammer toes well before then.

Price problems apart, it is getting harder every year to find well-designed shoes for children. The ideal shoe for a growing foot fastens with a lace or strap high over the instep, has a generously rounded toe and a low heel. There is no universally recognised ideal heel height, but in general 'the younger, the lower' is a good rule to follow.

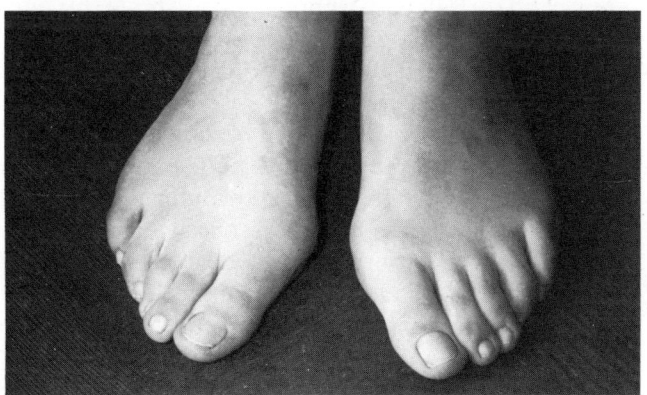

Feet of a thirteen-year-old girl with *hallux valgus* and crowding of the toes.

To avoid damage, shoes should be expertly fitted. When a child stands in a new shoe there should be half an inch of space between the end of the longest toe and the end of the shoe, and the shoe width should be correct. 'Weight-on' gauges are more accurate than the type the child does not have to stand on for measuring. Buying shoes a size too large is no solution – the foot slips forward, cramping the toes just as if the shoe was too small.

Children, girls especially, put enormous pressure on their mothers to buy fashionably styled shoes. Mothers are reluctant to insist, so there is a growing market for fashion shoes for children.

Consumer Action by MARGARET MCCURRIE
from *Labour Weekly*

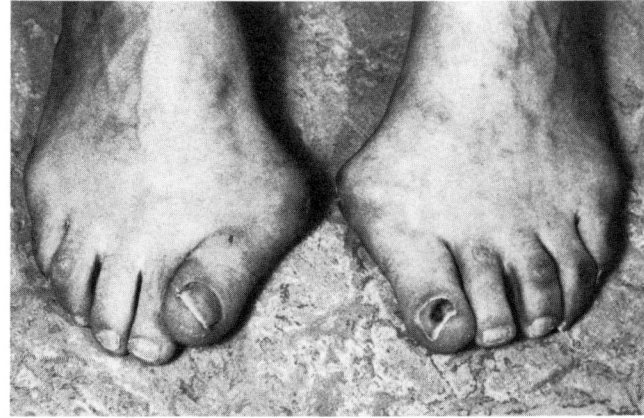

Feet of a seventy-year-old woman with severe *hallux valgus*.

3 Medical survey

Surveys have been carried out on children's feet and show that defects are equally common among boys and girls in early school years. Above this age, however, the proportion of girls with defective feet, in contrast to boys, becomes very much higher.

The commonest and most serious foot defect is *hallux valgus* – the turning of the big toe towards the others. After a while, a bunion will form on the big toe joint as it sticks out more and more from the inner edge of the foot; the forefoot splays but, unless specially made shoes are worn, the big toe keeps pushing the others out of position until, finally, the second toe's joint also often gives way. Pain, sometimes crippling, is the result. The only cure for extreme *hallux valgus* is surgery, and it is not always very successful.

One survey of school children showed that, at age 16, over half the girls were developing *hallux valgus*, while less than a sixth of the boys were.

So boys suffer much less, and barefoot people only occasionally. It is very probable that unsuitable shoes worn during a girl's adolescence are the main cause.

Much of the suffering among old age pensioners today – from flat feet, bunions, overriding toes, clawing corns, callosities, headaches, dizziness, irritability and sciatica – can be traced back to childhood footwear.

Research work

1 Carry out a survey of shoes worn by twelve boys and/or girls in your class. Write notes on their suitability in terms of the information supplied above. Mention any signs of *hallux valgus*.

2 *If the shoe fits*
Copy the chart below then fill in your priorities in the table by numbering the different considerations 1, 2, 3, etc.

	Football boot	Summer sandal	Indoor slipper	High Fashion shoe	Welling-ton boot	For the dance floor
fit						
warmth						
dryness						
protection						
cost						
appearance						
durability						

Further research

1 Consider the 1962 figures for various households as shown below. Copy them on to your own sheet of paper. Then find two or three similar households, and carry out interviews. Now make a similar chart headed with this year's date. Then compile a written report on the differences which emerge from your charts on the average spending per week on cakes in 1962 and this year.

1 Family Size and Cake Buying 1962
Average spending per household per week on cakes in pence

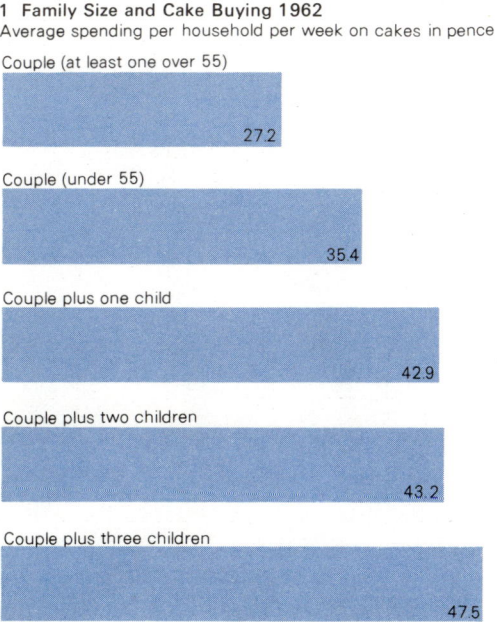

Couple (at least one over 55) — 27.2

Couple (under 55) — 35.4

Couple plus one child — 42.9

Couple plus two children — 43.2

Couple plus three children — 47.5

2 What Housewives Take into Account Most, When Making:

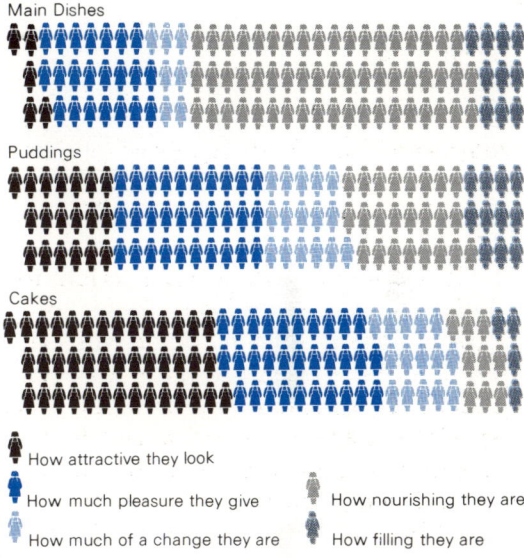

Main Dishes

Puddings

Cakes

How attractive they look

How much pleasure they give   How nourishing they are

How much of a change they are   How filling they are

2 Copy the chart onto your own sheet of paper. Then compile a report on the facts as presented on the chart. Head it: *Housewife's Choice*. Notice that each of the three blocks contains 100 people. This should enable you to express your report in terms of percentages under the headings: Main dishes, Puddings, and Cakes.

For your information

Sound films in colour: *Your feet*
Our children's feet
Both can be hired from Sound Services Ltd. Kingston Road, London SW19 3NR.
The foot and you is a filmstrip in black and white from The Health Education Council, Lynton House, 7/12 Tavistock Square, London WC1H 9LT.

Visual awareness

Examine the footwear in the photographs below.
1 Explain in what way any or all of the footwear shown may be out of date and unfashionable now.
2 In light of the information given at the beginning of this unit explain how some or all of the footwear shown may cause damage to the feet of the wearer.

Shops and shoes

Visit one or two local stores and/or shoe shops and
find out the answers to the questions below.
Work in small groups. It may be advisable to write
or telephone for an appointment in the first
instance.

1 What variety of *widths* are available in each size
  of shoe?
2 Has the manager of the shoe department seen a
  recent copy of The Children's Foot Health
  Register? (it is supported by the British Medical
  Association.)
3 Is the shop included in the Register?

4. Sportsview

Visual awareness and discussion

Work in small groups and choose three or four of these pictures and answer the questions which follow.

1 *Competition and stress*
This Olympic athlete is waiting for the start of the final – it might be called, *Competition and stress*. Describe his feelings and thoughts as he waits for the line-up. Discuss the best words to use.

2 *Show jump*
Study this picture of Olympic silver medallist Ann Moore. Describe her feelings at this dramatic moment – half way over the jump. Then make up a short story about a show jumping competition called, *Almost but not quite*. Begin, 'I really should have won that gold medal yesterday.' Now say in a few sentences how you think the horse feels at this moment as shown in Chris Smith's picture above.

4 *Tennis match*
Mixed doubles in the 1880s. Point out in what
ways it is different from 'Wimbledon' today.

3 *Swimming pool*
For your information this 16-year-old blonde,
Shane Gould from Sydney, Australia, is a triple
Olympic champion. She is seen here at the Crystal
Palace, London, in 1973.

Do you think everyone in the picture is con-
centrating on 'posing' for the photographer? What
do you think the girl and boy at the back on the
left are thinking as they gaze up at this world
famous champion?

On the air

You are a TV or radio commentator at the world's
finals of one of the sports shown in this unit.
Record, write, or speak your commentary. Lead
in with a few remarks on the personality and
background of some of the competitors. But you
have a time slot of only three minutes, so you need
to take up your commentary in the closing stages
of the event.

6 *Cricket match*

This cricket match probably took place in the year 1743. Describe in what ways it is different from a cricket match today Refer to the pitch, the equipment, the costume, the styles of batting and bowling, etc.

7 *All-in wrestling*

Tell the story of what happened before and after this heavyweight leap. Give it time and place and include descriptions of sounds and smells. Choose vivid words and phrases.

5 *Up and over!*

Notice how this photograph gives an impression of the spectators who form something of a pattern in the background. Describe what this athlete must now do to the pole. Then describe briefly the action of the run up to a pole vault and sensation of landing from the considerable height. What is the best way to 'fall' from a jump like this?

The poet speaks

All-in wrestlers

These two great men battling like lovers
Groan and pant in limbs that strangle,
Hold and abandon, clip and part.
Such is their longing for one another.
Each is the other's bitter angel,
Yet for love they wrestle, heart to heart.

They stand as close together
As those two young workmen, one of whom
Removes with the wetted corner of
His crumpled handkerchief a splinter
From his mate's left eye, a dumb
Show of man's concern for man, a silent love.

But then a leg is hooked, an arm once more
Is pressed beyond the limits of desire,
And one upon the other falls, who with a yell
Full of imploring anger beats the floor
With helpless fist, while his enemy, with cruel fire,
Grapples the loser to his breast, and screws him
　　into hell.

　　　　　　　　　JAMES KIRKUP (born 1923)

For information

The *Science Museum* South Kensington London
SW7 sell booklets on many aspects of flying, from
myth to space travel. Most are well illustrated
and cheap.

The flying fool

At eight minutes to eight on 20 May 1927 Lindbergh
coaxed his machine into the air above New York
airport. It was so heavily loaded with extra petrol
tanks that three times it bumped down again and
when it did eventually rise it only just cleared a
tractor standing in a field nearby. Lindbergh's
friends who watched the little silver monoplane
slowly disappear never expected to see its pilot
again. Then this very brave man began his lonely
flight of $33\frac{1}{2}$ hours, over Newfoundland, through the
fog and ice which had enveloped Alcock and Brown,
and on over Ireland and England to Paris. His two
greatest worries were that he would lose his way or
fall asleep. Actually he steered a very true course,
though once during the journey he flew low over the
water and asked a fisherman the way to Ireland.
Needless to say the surprised man was too amazed to
speak! When he landed at Le Bourget airport, Paris,
he still had enough petrol to fly another thousand
miles.

He had been sighted long before he ended his
heroic flight. One hundred thousand people crowded
to see him at 9.20 p.m. on the evening of 21 May,
and the exhausted man was almost frightened by his
tumultous reception. The French crowd went nearly
mad with excitement and pressed so closely round
the plane that he could hardly get out of his little
cabin. In the end a man had to put on Lindbergh's
helmet and pretend to be the flyer, whilst Lindbergh
himself made his escape into one of the hangars.

Americans are justly proud of Charles Lindbergh,
the 'Flying Fool' who first flew the Atlantic alone.

　　　L E SNELLGROVE *From Kitty Hawk to Outer Space*

Past history

1 *Olympic names*

In 1948 the Olympic games were held at Wembley. I sought one woman for her memories of those days: 'Yes, we went to Wembley three times. I was always keen on athletics; I hurdled at school; but I was 14 when the war came and that stopped it . . . I remember Fanny Blankers-Koen, the Dutch girl, with her blonde hair tied behind her back, and our own Maureen Gardner who so nearly beat her in the hurdles. I remember Maureen running off the track and being embraced by Geoff Dyson, the coach . . .' (They are now Mr and Mrs Dyson, living at Winchester.)

The 'Flying Dutchwoman' as Fanny Blankers-Koen quickly became known, was the heroine of the 1948 Games. This mother of two children won gold medals in the 100 metres, 200 metres, 80 metres hurdles and the sprint relay.

This was also the first opportunity in Britain to see Zatopek, the man who was to revolutionise distance running, and whose rolling ungainly style puzzled the experts. But there was no doubt of the man's ability when after nine laps of the 10 000 metres, Zatopek took off and broke his rivals with a searing burst of pace. With the rest of the field destroyed, he did not let up and although seeming to be in agony with every stride he pushed himself to an Olympic record of 29 min 59·6 sec with the next man three-quarters of a lap behind.

In the 5 000 metres he came from behind and with a tremendous burst across the last lap just failed by a fifth of a second to catch Gaston Rieff of Belgium. The athletic world, though, had been warned by the man in the red vest of Czechoslovakia; and four years later at Helsinki he pulled off the biggest Olympic coup with the gold medals in the 5 000 metres, 10000 metres and the Marathon.

There was the elegance of Jamaica's Arthur Wint

in the 400 metres, pulling back a deficit to take the gold medal from fellow countryman Herb McKinley. And there was the frail-looking British woman in the high jump: it was the last event on the last day and most of the crowd stayed to watch Dorothy Tyler battle in the event against Alice Couchman of the United States. Both women cleared 5ft 6½in, a new Olympic record; but the American woman took the gold because she had fewer failures than Mrs Tyler: which was exactly how the British woman had lost the Olympic title in Berlin, 12 years before, when she was 16-year-old Dorothy Odam.

The Marathon had its drama with Etienne Gally of Belgium having run almost 26 miles, entering the Stadium through the tunnel to a tumultuous roar only to totter and stagger painfully through the last 500 yards and to be passed, first by Delfo Cabrera of Argentina and then by Ron Richards of Britain. The decathlon, that extreme test of stamina and skill, was won by a 17-year-old American, Bob Mathias, who broke the world record.

But the best Wembley Olympic story for me concerns the men's 4 by 100 metres relay. The Americans won it by the proverbial street only to be disqualified for a faulty baton change. The crowd, 83 000 that day, had a chance to cheer Britain's first gold medal of the Games: but the cheers were for the Americans. The British did not want to win on a disqualification. The Americans lodged a protest and sought the evidence of the official film-maker. A man called Harold Conrad spent two days chasing round London getting the crucial piece of film developed. The jury of appeal looked at it, saw that no foul had been committed and awarded the Olympic title to the US.

Conrad has moved from film making to professional boxing and has been closely connected with Muhammad Ali's recent fights: Ali of course was the Olympic light heavyweight boxing champion of the Rome Games in 1960 just three years before that June night when he was dumped on his pants by a left hook from Henry Cooper; that of course is another piece of Wembley history.

JOHN RODDA *The Guardian*

Group work: history today

Find out some more recent history about spectacular events or famous personalities in sport today – either nationally or locally. Work in groups; choose one or two sporting activities, then tape a report on some interesting happenings based on your research.

You could also collect newspaper cuttings and photographs to make a poster collage for display in the classroom. Or compile your own scrapbook.

2 *Wembley story:* The White Horse
Fifty years ago the first FA Cup Final at Wembley between Bolton Wanderers and West Ham United was played on 28 April 1923 – just four days after the Stadium was opened. It was an extraordinary day. Without any yardstick to go on, the Stadium authorities had set their capacity crowd at 127 000 – and then sat back on 'the day' ready to sell their tickets at the turnstiles. And inside a few hours over half a million people turned up – about 200 000 of them, the figure will never be known, getting inside the Stadium.

It could have been an unmitigated disaster. There had been little opportunity for the builders to test the structure for safety beforehand, though they did employ an infantry battalion from Chelsea Barracks to run up and down the terraces with packs on their backs in the weeks before completion.

But no one had given a thought to limiting the crowd. The Final of the year before had been watched by only 53 000 at Stamford Bridge and the Stadium authorities, reasonably, now expected no more than double that figure, comfortable for the largest stadium in the world. They never even considered making the match all-ticket.

The sun shone from dawn. Before 1 p.m. the police and Stadium authorities realised they had misread things; by 2 p.m. with the trains and buses still disgorging thousands, the doors were locked and the turnstile men took flight. So the crowd went at the fences. By 3 p.m., when the match was meant to start, virtually the whole of the playing area was covered.

Then the Man on the White Horse rode his way into the legend. Constable G A Scorey, of the mounted police division, once told his story: 'Whatever credit there was went to Billie, my horse. It was the first time he really behaved himself too . . . I was in the detachment of mounted police held in reserve about four miles from the Stadium. We weren't expecting to be called on. I know I was thinking about my wedding and not about football. It was about 2.30 that we got the order to mount. We arrived at Wembley about the time kickoff was due with orders to clear the pitch. Clear the pitch! You couldn't see it! I felt like giving up; there was nobody in charge I could see and I just didn't know where to start.

'Anyway Billie knew what to do. He pushed forward quietly and the crowd made way for him. He answered all my orders beautifully and, although it was hard work, the crowd seemed to respect the horse. I told them to link hands and push away from the touchline. Inside half an hour the job was done and the match started. I stopped there, of course, although I can't remember much about the game; as I say, I wasn't very keen on football and have never seen a match since.'

The teams had been kept in the dressing-room but at 3.40 they were told to risk it – heaven knows what would have happened had the authorities called off the game – and they funnelled out through a passage made by the remarkably good natured multitude.

They were introduced to the King. Then, as Ted Vizard the Bolton outside left, later wrote: 'It felt as though we were playing in a human box. The game started and within a few minutes we were one up. I shall never forget David Jack's shot flashing past Ted Hufton . . . when I was taking corners I had to tell the crowds, "Let me lean on you, give me a push, and perhaps I'll get the ball near the goal." . . . Later, cutting in down the goal line, I saw J R Smith running into position. As he fastened on to my centre I watched him screw the ball into the net before the West Ham defenders knew what was happening. Few realised at once what had happened because the ball bounced straight back into play

from the mass of spectators wedged against the back of the net.' So Bolton won by 2–0.

Wembley did not get a very good press next day. The *Sunday Pictorial* for instance had an editorial: 'The much vaunted Wembley Stadium has shown up very badly in its first test. Yesterday's Final seems to have been a fiasco of the most appalling sort.'

In the following week questions were asked in the Commons. And, of course, the inevitable inquiry was set up. One member (Mr F O Roberts) drew cheers from the House when he asked: 'Is the Home Secretary aware of the almost universal praise of the conduct of the police, especially of the officer who was mounted on a white horse?'

And what of Constable Scorey? He is now dead. But *The Guardian's* own football correspondent, Eric Todd, once memorably interviewed him. He recalled returning his horse to the stable the evening after the match, then calling round to see his fiancée, Kitty. She asked him what sort of day he had had, 'Oh, just ordinary, lass. Just ordinary.'

FRANK KEATING *The Guardian*

Words at work

Paragraph 1 (page 40)
What is: *a yardstick, a capacity crowd*?
Describe *a turnstile*.
Paragraph 2 (page 40)
What is: *an unmitigated disaster, an infantry battalion*?
Paragraph 3 (page 40)
About how many people did the stadium authorities expect at Wembley in 1923?
Paragraph 4 (page 41)
Look up the meaning of *disgorging* in a dictionary.
Paragraph 5 (page 41)
What is a *legend*? Explain *a detachment of mounted police*. Now find six vivid words and phrases from the rest of this article. Choose two of them and use each in a sentence of your own.

Character study

Write one paragraph describing the character of Constable G A Scorey.

Short story

Try your hand at a dramatic short story. Use one of the following as your opening sentence if you wish.
The cell door slammed shut.
He seemed calm but I noticed his knuckles were
    white where he was gripping the rail.
'You're next!' My heart sank.
I had not expected such a complete silence.

Let's get the facts

'Football developed as a regulated team game after formation of Football Association in 1863. The game is played between 2 teams of eleven players in a field 100–130 yards by 50–100 yards, marked by lines. The object is to propel a round leather ball into the opposing goal, an area 8 yards wide and 8 feet high, without use of hands or arms.

The field has a half-way line, a 10 yd. radius centre circle, two penalty areas (each 44 yd. by 6 yd.). Corner kicks are taken from a one yard segment, when the ball goes behind the goal-line off a defender. For major offences committed within a defender's penalty area, a penalty kick may be awarded by the referee to the attacking team. This is taken 12 yd. from the goal centre, with only the goalkeeper within the area. The game is started from the centre spot and continues for 90 minutes. After a half-time interval the teams change ends. The team scoring the most goals is the winner!

1 Write a similar accurate and factual description of one of these team games: cricket, rugby football, ice-hockey, hockey, lawn tennis, table tennis, lacrosse, netball.
(Use almost the same number of words, about 170.)

2 Describe some of the 'major offences' for which a penalty is awarded in the game you have just described.

3 The 'Off-side' rule was omitted from the above description. Either explain its main points in your own words or explain the off-side rule as it applies to the game you have just described.

4 Describe one of the following exactly: skis, a cricket bat, a tennis racquet, a hockey stick, a fishing rod, ice skates.

Further research – An optional extra for those who have time to spare.

You may have time and interest to work on one of these subjects. You could then transfer your findings to your folder work as part of your folio of writing for this year.
    Give an account, with maps, pictures and diagrams where appropriate, of *one* of the following:
    The first four minute mile   Channel swimming
    Decathlon and Pentathlon   The Marathon
    Blood sports   Women in sport
    World figure skating   Gymnastics display
    Show jumping

Physical fitness: the Harvard Step Test

Work in groups and record individual performances in this Harvard Step Test. This is one example:

1 Stand erect in front of a bench 381 mm high.
2 Place one foot on bench and step up until both feet are full on bench with legs straight and body erect (Count 1 and 2).
3 Step down one foot at a time (Count 3 and 4).
4 Carry on for 5 minutes at the rate of one ascent (4 counts) per two seconds, i.e. a total of 150 ascents.

Note:
Variations can be used, e.g. only 30 ascents and/or a lower bench height.

Now take 3 pulse(P) counts as follows:
Take P.1 $1\frac{1}{2}$ minutes after completion of exercise.
Take P.2 $2\frac{1}{2}$ minutes after completion of exercise.
Take P.3 $4\frac{1}{2}$ minutes after completion of exercise.
The Physical Fitness Index (PFI) is calculated as follows:

$$\frac{15\,000}{P.1 + P.2 + P.3}$$

Note:
1 There may be important *medical* reasons why some people should *not* take part in the Harvard Step Test or other physical exercise. Check in your group before starting work.
2 Emil Zatopek (see *Olympic names* passage on page 39) achieved a PFI of 172 using a 508 mm bench.

Research projects – Work in small groups

1 What is the first known date of the Olympic Games?
2 When were they abolished by the Emperor Theodosius?
3 When did Baron Pierre de Coubertin revive them?
4 When were women admitted to the Games?
5 'The important thing is not to win but to take part.' Is this true of the Olympics? Is this true of all sport?
6 Bring this table up to date for the years since 1968:
Women's 100 Metres World Record

1934	11·7 seconds	1955	11·3 seconds
1937	11·6 seconds	1962	11·2 seconds
1948	11·5 seconds	1965	11·1 seconds
1952	11·4 seconds	1968	11·0 seconds

7 The Olympic flag symbolises the five continents of the globe. Sketch and colour its design and name the continents.

An oar for Women's Lib

8 With women's rowing in the Olympic Games for the first time in 1976, find out about the career of Miss Chuter, a leading coach. Explain the meaning of the caption to this picture of Penny Chuter.
9 Argue the case against those who say, 'Why run when you can walk?' i.e. Is there any point in taking part in athletics (apart from health considerations)?

This sporting life

Fifteen minutes of the first half passed and I'd never even touched the ball. I was aching with activity and blowing hard. It took me most of the first half to realize I was being starved of the ball by my own team.

It was the hooker, Taff Gower, who was organising it, I decided; a quiet little frog working out his last days in the game with the 'A' team. With his scarred, toothless face, his short bow-legged figure stumped alongside me in each movement and casually diverted the ball whenever it came my way. I gathered he mustn't like me. I might be keeping one of his mates out of the team, stopping a wage. I didn't worry about this. I just saw an early end to my ambitions. As we folded down for the next scrum his face was further forward than mine. 'Why're you keeping the ball from me?' I asked him. His head was upside down, waiting for the ball to come in, but he was grinning fairly politely. I could see the back of his throat. When he spat I couldn't move my head. I didn't think he could like me.

I waited three scrums, to make him feel relaxed and also to get the best opportunity. I kept my right arm loose. His face was upside down, his eyes straining, loose in their sockets, to catch a glimpse of the ball as it came in. I watched it leave the scrum-half's hands and his head buckled under the forwards' heaving. I swung my right fist into the middle of his face. He cried out loud. I hit him again and saw the red pulp on his nose and lips as my hand came away. He was crying out really loud now, partly affected, professional pain, but most of it real. His language echoed all over the ground.

The scrum broke up with the ref blowing his nut off on the whistle. 'I saw that! I saw that!' he shouted, urged on to violent mimes of justice by the crowd's tremendous booing. They were all on their feet demonstrating and screaming. Gower had covered his face with his hands, but blood seeped between his fingers, as the trainer and two players directed his blind steps off the field.

'You'll be nailed for good for this, you dirty little swine. You'll never play again,' and all that, the ref was shouting. He pointed with real drama at the opposing hooker. The crowd's response reached a crescendo – far more than it would provide for, say, the burning of a church.

The young hooker shook his head. 'I ne'er touched him,' he said, looking round for support from his own team. 'I swear to God I never touched him.'

'You can tell that to the League Chairman.'

The hooker was beside himself with innocence. 'Nay, look at my bloody fist,' he said, 'Look, there's no blood on it.'

'I'm not arguing.'

The ref took his name and sent him off.

I'd never seen such a parade before. The whole ground throbbed with rage as the young figure in his little boy's costume passed in front of the main stand.

'They're not fit to be on a football field,' the ref said to me, since I happened to be standing nearest.

DAVID STOREY *This Sporting Life* (born 1933)

For discussion

In which instances in *This Sporting Life* account above did the players depart from the accepted ideas and rules governing 'sportsmanship'? In what ways do players and crowds break the rules in soccer matches?

Composition

Write a vivid description of a short, dramatic incident at one of the following:
an ice-hockey match; a motor cycle race;
a swimming or athletic relay race.

Outside broadcast

You are a BBC radio commentator. Tape or report either the David Storey incident or the one in your own composition.

Safety code for holiday climbers

Most accidents occur because those involved have underestimated the British hills. Too many inexperienced people insist on 'doing' Snowdon or Ben Nevis, no matter how treacherous the conditions.

Even at Easter, Snowdon can be transformed into a wilderness of snow (see picture).

Such people are not really interested in the mountains; they just want to brag when they get home. In fact there is nothing to brag about. If, through their stupidity, such people have an accident and the mountain rescue teams are called out to save them, then they can put other people's lives in unnecessary danger.

If you observe the following 'dos' and 'don'ts' you will be less likely to come to grief, and more likely to enjoy your mountain holidays:

1 Always go with at least one experienced companion.
2 Wear suitable windproof and waterproof clothes and walking boots, *not* shoes.
3 Take food and first-aid kit for emergencies.
4 Check the weather forecast before you set out.
5 Always take a map and compass, and know how to use them.
6 Leave word of your proposed route with a responsible person and tell him when you are safely back – otherwise the mountain rescue team may be called out unnecessarily.
7 Know when to turn back. It is not brave to push on regardless. It is just plain stupidity.
8 Do not go into the hills in winter. The weather can worsen rapidly, the days are short and it can be very cold.

9 Never go where there is snow or ice. Both are dangerous and can persist well into the Easter holidays.

If you would like to visit the mountains, but know of no one to take you, then perhaps the answer is one of the Mountaincraft holidays for 11- to 15-year-olds run by the Youth Hostels Association.

Research work (Refer to *film notes* on page 50 and make a study of one of the Hillcraft skills. Use books as well.)

1 Explain how useful a compass can be when mountaineering.
2 Give examples of conditions when it is safer for you to turn back.
3 Explain what to do if you and your companions get lost in a blizzard.
4 What food would you take with you on a mountain expedition lasting three days?
5 Find a recording of Moussorgsky's *Night on the bare mountain* and listen to its story.

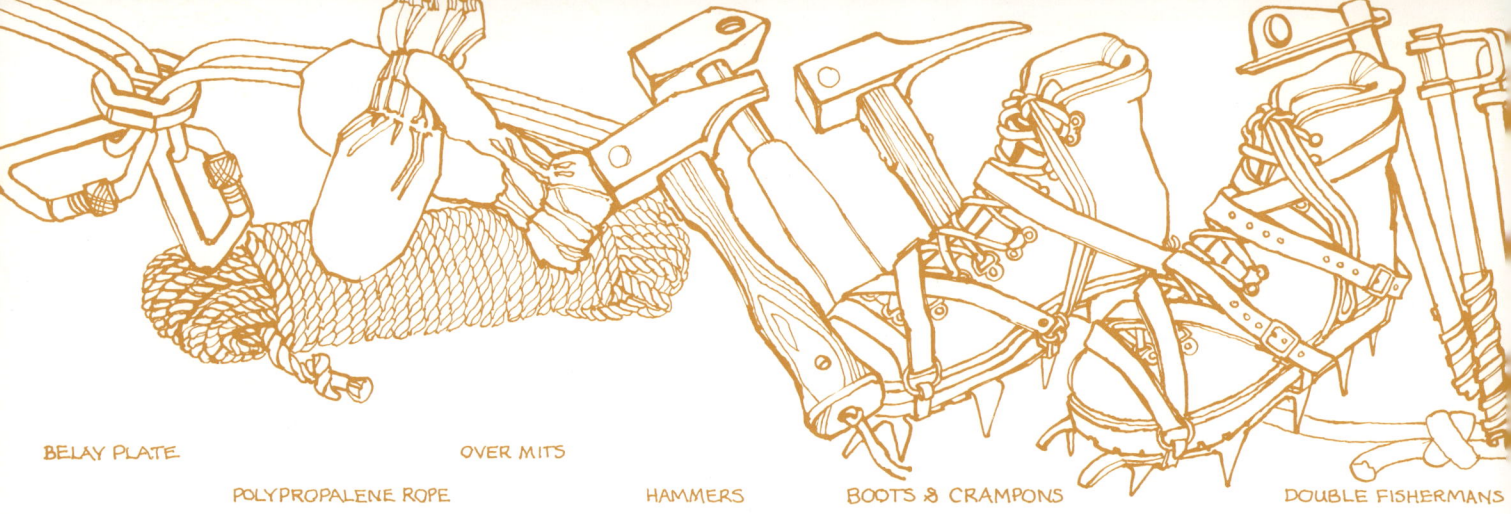

BELAY PLATE   OVER MITS

POLYPROPALENE ROPE   HAMMERS   BOOTS & CRAMPONS   DOUBLE FISHERMANS

The first very severe

Gwen Moffat was the first woman guide in Britain. Read this extract from her book *Space Below My Feet* two or three times. Then answer the questions which follow.

We had gone to Glyder Fach to do the Direct: that old-fashioned mountaineering route of splendid and varied situations; never really hard, never easy – and when we came to the point where the route goes left by way of the Toe and Finger traverse, I looked up, at the shallow trough of Gibson's Chimney, rising smooth and vertical above us.

'That's a VS,' I observed.

He studied it solemnly.

'Do you want to do it?' he asked.

'Yes.'

He looked at it more closely, then looked at the belay, – and me.

'But I want to lead it,' I said.

'Have you done it before?'

'No.'

'Have you led a VS before?'

'No.'

'Then I'll do it first.'

Secretly I was amused at this attitude of masculine superiority, although I would have taken it seriously had he been a tiger.

He had some shrapnel in one leg – a war wound, and I was a little anxious when he reached the crux and had to straddle the chimney, which is too shallow for comfort. But he heaved himself upwards, grunting, and discovered a large finishing hold on top. I

followed without any difficulty, and we descended the amusing little hand traverse at the side, then the Toe and Finger traverse, to return to our original position below the chimney.

I looked up. It hadn't changed. It was as if I'd never climbed it. I put the rope round my back, still staring. And before I started to move I felt the familiar feeling that came when I was about to do something hard. A mental and physical relaxation, a loosening of the muscles so complete that even the face relaxes and the eyes widen; one's body becomes light and supple – a pliable and co-ordinated entity to be shown a climb as a horse is shown a jump.

In that exquisite moment before the hard move, when one looks and understands, may lie an answer to the question why one climbs. You are doing something hard, so hard that failure could mean death, but because of knowledge and experience you are doing it safely. This safety depends on yourself; there is no other factor: no horse or piece of machinery to let you down. What you accomplish is by your own efforts, and the measure of your success is the width of your margin of safety.

GWEN MOFFAT *Space Below My Feet*

Words at work

Explain the meaning of these words as used in the above passage:

    traverse   trough   chimney   vertical

    shallow   supple   pliable   co-ordinated

Explain the use of inverted commas (quotation marks) in the dialogue. What punctuation *rules* apply?

47

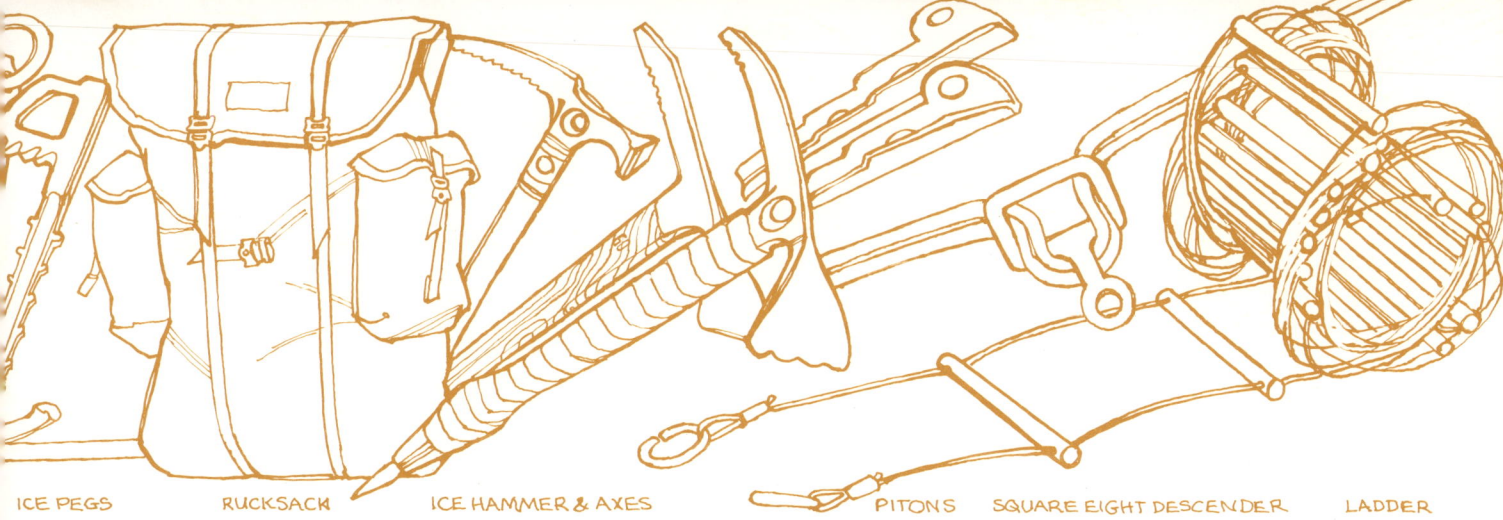

ICE PEGS   RUCKSACK   ICE HAMMER & AXES   PITONS   SQUARE EIGHT DESCENDER   LADDER

End of a climb

It was eight o'clock when I mantelshelfed on the top of the cornice and stood up in the moonlight. Eight o'clock and the valleys dark, and the lights of villages gleaming in Italy. We had spent twelve hours on the ridge.

We came straight down the Verra glacier to turn the southern spur of the Breithorn. Below, in the dimness, we could see vague troughs and domes softened by moonlight. It was very cold and we were tired. It needed a lot of willpower to concentrate on the snow as we walked, watching for the thin lines of hidden crevasses.

We came under the spur and started the long uphill climb to the Breithorn Pass. As we gained height the wind increased – a north wind, bitterly cold.

We came to the level ridge and there were no more crevasses and we walked side by side. Occasionally we stopped to examine each other's faces by torchlight, looking for signs of frostbite.

My senses were a little dulled and life held no problems. Life was the sound of crampons scrunching the snow, the lights of the refuge coming up, and Life was the power and the glory of all the mountains I had ever climbed – as I walked along the frontier in the moonlight.

GWEN MOFFAT *Space Below My Feet*

What was it that required a lot of willpower and concentration? Why was this requirement so necessary on the Southern spur of the Breithorn?

Words at work

Use a dictionary as necessary and explain the meaning of these words as used in this passage.

mantelshelfed cornice glacier spur troughs domes crevasse frostbite crampons scrunching refuge frontier concentration

Comprehension

1 Read the first passage again, then in your own words give Gwen Moffat's answer to the question *Why one climbs*.
2 Give each of the Gwen Moffat articles another title.

Research work

1 How many minutes of BBC 1 TV time will be devoted to sports events from next Monday to Sunday inclusive? Name each sport and the time allocated to it.
2 Give a brief description of the game of Squash.
3 Find out why Emily Davidson threw herself under the feet of the King's horse racing in the Derby at Epsom in 1913.
4 What is a *cyclocross championship*?

Composition

Either write a short description of the training routine necessary for any one sport, or write a short appreciation of those sports which are non-competitive and followed 'just for the fun of it'.

The poet speaks

Climbing

The branch swayed, swerved,
Swept and whipped, up,
Down, right to left,
Then leapt to the right again,
As if to hurl him down
To smash to smithereens
On the knife-edge grass
Or smother
In the close-knit quilts of moss.
Out on a crazy limb
He screwed his eyes tight shut,
To keep out the dizzy ground.
Sweat greased his palms;
Fear pricked his forehead.
The twisted branches lunged and lurched,
His body curved, twisted, he arched
His legs and gripped the bark
Between his ankles.
The crust of the bark
Sharp as glasspaper
And rough with wrinkles
Grazed his skin
And raised the raw red flesh
And crazed his mind
With fear of breaking.
Then the mad-cap, capering wind
Dropped.
The branch steadied,
Paused,
Rested.
He slowly clambered, slowly, back,
Slowly to safety,
Then dropped
Like a wet blanket
To the rock-like, reassuring ground.
Finally, without a sound,
He walked carefully
Home.

GEOFFREY SUMMERFIELD

Last words

1 By Tao-Yun (AD 400)
High rises the Eastern Peak
Soaring up to the blue sky.
Among the rocks – an empty hollow,
Secret, still, mysterious!
Uncarved and unknown,
Screened by nature with a roof of clouds.
Times and seasons, what things are you
Bringing to my life ceaseless change?
I will lodge for ever in his hollow
Where springs and autumns unheeded pass.

2 By the Chinese professor
'Sir, sir! Nurmi's clipped 2·2 seconds off the world
mile record', a California student exclaimed one
day in 1923 as he burst into the philosophy class.
The Chinese professor nodded understandingly and
asked: 'What does the honourable Finnish gentle-
man intend to do with the time he has saved?'

3 Why do you want to climb it?
'Because it is there', answered George Leigh
Mallory.

Further reading

TSCHIFFELY *The Tale of Two Horses* Hodder
W B MCMORRIS *Mountaineering* Dobson
E SHIPTON *Mountain Conquest* Caravel
R BRASCH *How Did Sports Begin?* Longman
F D OMMANNEY *South Latitude* Longman
GERALD DURRELL *The Bafut Beagles* Hart Davies
SIR JOHN HUNT *The Ascent of Everest* Allen & Unwin

HERMAN MELVILLE *Moby Dick* Dent
NATIONAL WESTMINSTER BANK *Coaching Series*
　Bailey Bros.
SHEILA WILCOX *Three Days Running* Collins
Know The Game Series published by Educational
　Productions, Wakefield, Yorkshire.
ECKER & WILT *Illustrated Guide to Olympic Techniques*
　Faber
S STYLES *Modern Mountaineering* Faber
Rock Climbing published by Educational
　Productions　　　　　　　　　　　.
GWEN MOFFAT *Space Below My Feet* Hodder
WITTS & WOOD *Athletics for the '70s* Arthur Barker
FOSTER *The Experience of Sport* Longman

Film notes

Hillcraft 1 Going to the Hills – sound film
　black and white 17 mins.
Hillcraft 2 Leading in the Hills – sound film
　colour 15 mins
Hillcraft 3 Camping in the Hills – sound film
　colour 12 mins.
Hillcraft 4 Survival in the Hills – sound film
　colour 18 mins.
All from Explorer Films, 58 Stratford Road,
Bromsgrove, Wilts.

The Camper and his Equipment
The Campsite
Fires and Cooking (in camp)
Filmstrips in colour from Sound Services Ltd.,
Kingston Road, London SW19 3NR.
Wrestling – 30 minutes – BFI

5. Language study one

This is the first of three short Language study units in this book (see also pages 83 and 125). The work set here revises some of the more formal language and vocabulary skills needed, when the time comes, to tackle Test Papers and examinations. In fact, most essential aspects of this work are contained within the other units, but as a check on skills so far acquired, here are a few 'out of context' studies.

Definition and factual description

Consider this definition: A *pen* is an implement with a metal nib which is used for writing.

A definition must be a brief but clear statement of fact. It should name the *class* to which the word to be defined belongs and then make a distinction between that object and others in its class.

1 Criticise the following attempts at definition:
A *window* is an oblong glass part of the wall of a house that you can see through.
A *wheelbarrow* is to take things from one field to another.
A *horse* is an animal without horns but having four legs, used for hunting and farm work.

2 Assign each of the following words printed in capital letters to its correct group from the list printed below, e.g. VIOLIN: instrument
HAPPINESS BICYCLE MOTH SAW
WASTE-PAPER BASKET BREAST STROKE LATHE
KNIFE CARTON BOOK-KEEPING
Implement Container System Receptacle
Tool Emotion Method Machine Vehicle
Insect

3 Now briefly complete the definition of each of the above words by adding its distinguishing feature,
e.g. VIOLIN: a *stringed* instrument for *making music*.

4 A factual description is essentially an expanded form of a definition. Read the passage below and notice how it develops from the first sentence:

THE HEART is a muscular organ which acts as a pump. It is situated in the chest behind the breast-bone and ribs, between the lungs and immediately above the diaphragm; it lies with a quarter of its bulk to the right, and the remaining three-quarters to the left of the middle line of the body. Its beat may be felt just below and to the inner side of the left breast. The heart has four cavities, two on either side of a central partition. *Arteries* convey the blood from the heart; *veins* carry it to the heart.

Punctuation

Punctuate the following passage carefully, paying special attention to apostrophes:

its peculiar how peoples intelligence varies even after five years work theres still doubt where to place the apostrophes take the word its can you be certain if theres one at all a good rule to remember is that if it means it is its spelt its everyones punctuation needs care after all its ill mannered to be slovenly in writing just as it is to be sloppy in dress and to mumble your speech

Rewrite with the correct paragraphing and punctuation:

the dragon looked up at st george and with a coy giggle said i say would you mind removing your lance from my ribs it tickles cant you go and prod a windmill or something sorry old chap id like to oblige but thats don quixotes job it needs special training just be patient ive got my job to do and if you keep still it will soon be over well youre wasting your time said the dragon with a superior smile didnt you know im just a figment of your imagination surely you dont believe all that stuff about dragons we dont exist

Dictionary work

Find out the meaning and use of these grammatical terms:

prefix   suffix   adjective   verb
indirect speech   inverted commas

Notice that many adjectives carry several different meanings or shades of meaning: e.g.

BRIGHT: beaming   blazing   brilliant   gleaming
burnished   glossy   lustrous   sunny
intelligent   sparkling

Use the word *bright* as an adjective in ten separate sentences so that each illustrates one of the meanings listed above.

Now use *brightly* and *brightness* in two separate sentences of your own.

Looking at words

1 In exercises involving description of a technical process, economy in the number of words used and a precise choice are required. In the following, find the *exact word* for each description, e.g.

A substance that is easily bent to a desired shape: PLIABLE
A substance that will not bend:
A substance composed of small grains:
A liquid that bubbles with gas:
A substance that will not dissolve in water:
A substance that will burn readily:
A process that occurs by itself without man's aid:
A substance that floats easily and refuses to sink:
An article in the shape of:
a cylinder   a sphere   a cube   a globe
a triangle   a cone

2 By adding a prefix, or changing the suffix, form words *opposite* to:

prudent   audible   perceptible   legible
graceless   merciful   pure   thrifty
thankless   mobile   active   gracious

3 Write two quite separate sentences for each word below to show two distinct meanings:

file   lock   coach   ruler

4 Find five other words which have two distinct meanings. Use each in a sentence of your own.

5 Give examples of your own to explain *prefix* and *suffix*.

Words in character

1 In the passage below, the words in italics give an unfavourable impression of the character they describe. Copy out the passage, replacing the words in italics with a selection of those from the list provided, so as to give an entirely *favourable* impression:

My great aunt Matilda was *extravagant* in her ways. Although not generous to her poor nephews, she was always finding *pretexts* for *wasting* her inheritance. She was eccentric, however, in one respect. She was *notorious* for the *antiquated* cars she drove in. But old though they were, she was *fussy* about their appearance and was perpetually *wheedling* the *gruff* old village store-keeper into acquiring *new-fangled* polishes. These were frequently needed, because she was *foolhardy* enough in her driving to be more off the road than on it.

renowned	novel	up-to-date	persuading
bluff	dashing	lavish	veteran
derelict	meticulous	reputed	dare-devil
pretences	squandering	occasions	churlish
prodigal	inducing	circumspect	spending

2 Study this list of main features of a character in a play:
HAIR: scanty, lifeless; EYES: shifty, watery; BUILD: lean; CLOTHES: shabby, threadbare; EXPRESSION: discontented.
Now write a paragraph of 100 words describing his first entry on to the stage.

3 Draw up a similar list describing a person who is different in every way.

4 Now write a paragraph of 75 words describing her first entry onto the stage.

5 Draw up a list of words to describe some famous person. Ask others to identify your choice.

6 Draw up a list of words to describe yourself in five years time.

7 Mime one of the characters from questions 2, 3, 5, or 6 above.

Direct and indirect speech

1 Consider the following:
He said that he could ask him.
The speaker said that he could ask his friend.
The speaker said that he could ask John Smith.
Explain why the second and third sentences are clearer than the first.
Study these helpful guides for Indirect Speech:
No inverted commas are used.
All verbs are put into past tense.
If the verbs are already in the past tense, they are carried one stage further back (e.g. *saw* becomes *had seen*).
All pronouns change to the third person.
For accuracy and variety, the 'saying' word is carefully chosen and reflects the *tone* of the original speech, e.g. he snarled, he suggested.
Certain adverbs of time are changed from the present, e.g. *today, tomorrow, yesterday,* to more distant phrases,
on that day, the next day, the day before.

2 Consider the following examples of Direct and Indirect (or Reported) Speech.
'I wonder, John, if you would be good enough to move your feet off the chair. I would rather like to sit down now.'
He said that he wondered if John would have been good enough to take his feet off the chair. He would have liked to sit down then.
In what way is the use of *would have* and *then* somewhat ridiculous and unnatural?
Now consider this alternative version in Indirect Speech. In what way is this more natural and polite?
John's visitor politely asked him to remove his feet from the chair, as he wished to sit down.

3 Write the following in direct speech:
The fruit was his, he said, and he would be glad if I would return it at once. He was sure that my mother would be very upset and that my father would punish me severely. He asked why I had done it. However, he concluded, he might decide not to tell my parents if I would apologise immediately.

4 Now examine these examples:

'What the devil are you doing?' the instructor shouted. 'Can't you even change the gears yet! A ten year old boy could manage them better than you. Now . . . take a deep breath, count ten, and we'll start again.'

The instructor shouted and asked what on earth the pupil was doing. He asked whether he couldn't even change the gears yet. He went on to say that a ten year old boy could have managed better than him. He finally asked the pupil to take a deep breath, count ten and then said that they would start again.

5 Now compare the version below and discuss which is the closer in *tone* to the direct speech:

(With quite a show of temper) the driving instructor asked what on earth the pupil was doing, suggesting (scornfully) that a ten year old could have managed the gears better. (When he had recovered his patience) he (pleaded) with the pupil to take a deep breath, (relax) and then they would try again.

6 Rewrite the following passage of indirect speech as direct speech, paying careful attention to paragraphing and punctuation:

His father informed John with a look of disgust on his face and a hint of sarcasm in his voice, that it was difficult to change the back wheel of the car on to the front at the same time because they had only one jack. His son John made a helpful suggestion. Perhaps it would be possible to prop up one end with bricks. The father was delighted with the boy's brilliant idea and turning towards him a face dangerous in its sweetness asked where he was expected to find four bricks on the middle of Dartmoor. John murmured that he thought his father knew all there was to know about that particular subject, but that if he had forgotten, he himself was a little more organised, even though he was an apparent imbecile of fifteen, whereupon he went to the boot of the car and produced the required bricks to his father's great astonishment.

7 Put the following conversation into indirect speech:

'What on earth made you think of putting those bricks in the boot, John?' asked his father a few minutes later.

'I remember last year's holiday tour,' replied John, with some feeling. 'I seemed to spend all my time knocking at people's doors asking if they could lend me some bricks because the car jack was too short, or water because the radiator was leaky.'

'Well we're all right this time, son, thanks to you. I'll just put some air into the spare wheel and get the wheel brace . . .'

Unfortunately something had been left behind to make room for the bricks.

Letter writing

1 Look again at Unit 4 *Sportsview* and choose one of the people in the photograph (on page 36) at the Crystal Palace Swimming Pool. Then write a letter as from the person you choose giving a short account of the occasion. You are writing to your Grandfather. Include some information about Shane Gould, and give your school address at the top of your letter.
2 You are a spectator on the occasion shown in *Sportsview* (Unit 4, All-in wrestling). Write a short letter to your aunt in Canada describing the scene in the photograph.

General rules

1 Give some general rules regarding the writing of direct speech, with particular reference to the use of inverted commas and to paragraphing.
2 Give some general rules to cover the main considerations when changing direct speech into indirect speech.
3 Give some general rules, with examples, for use of the full stop and the comma.

6. Countryside notebook

At the brook

Read this passage and answer the questions which follow:

Miners, single, trailing and in groups, passed like shadows diverging home. At the end of the ribbed level of sidings squat a low cottage, three steps down from the cinder track. A large bony vine clutched at the house, as if to claw down the tiled roof. Round the bricked yard grew a few wintry primroses. Beyond, the long garden sloped down to a bush-covered brook course. There were some twiggy apple trees, winter-crack trees, and ragged cabbages. Beside the path hung dishevelled pink chrysanthemums, like pink cloths hung on bushes. A woman came stepping out of the felt-covered fowl-house, half-way down the garden. She closed and padlocked the door, then drew herself erect, having brushed some bits from her white apron.

She was a tall woman of imperious mien, handsome, with definite black eyebrows. Her smooth black hair was parted exactly. For a few moments she stood steadily watching the miners as they passed along the railway; then she turned towards the brook course. Her face was calm and set, her mouth was closed in disillusionment. After a moment she called:

'John!' There was no answer. She waited, and then said distinctly:

'Where are you?'

'Here!' replied a child's sulky voice from among the bushes. The woman looked piercingly through the dusk.

'Are you at that brook?' she asked sternly.

For answer the child showed himself before the raspberry-canes that rose like whips. He was a small, sturdy boy of five. He stood quite still, defiantly.

'Oh!' said the mother, conciliated. 'I thought you were down at that brook – and you remember what I told you –'

The boy did not have an answer.

'Come, come on in,' she said more gently, 'it's getting dark. There's your grandfather's engine coming down the line!'

D H LAWRENCE *Odour of Chrysanthemums* (1885–1930)

Interpretation and discussion

1 Using your dictionary, make sure you know what the words *diverging*, *dishevelled* and *conciliated* mean. Then explain: How are the miners *diverging*? Explain in your own words how chrysanthemums look when they are *dishevelled*, and hang *like pink cloths hung on bushes*. Draw these if you wish. Why is the mother *conciliated*?
2 What is the vine like, and what does it seem to be doing? What time of year is it? Find your evidence from the passage, and quote at least three reasons why you think it is this particular season. Why do you think the writer says the raspberry canes *rose like whips*?
3 Why does she speak 'more gently' at last? Write a story or a description, about this mother and this little boy. If you like you can pretend to be either of them. You may, if you like, continue their conversation.

For your information: Spaghetti Junction

This Gravelly Hill interchange (Birmingham)
covers 30 acres on which 130 buildings once stood.

Sport with a difference

Most of our national sports do not combine an immediately apparent usefulness with their competitive aspect. Knocking a ball over a net or down a little hole in the ground hardly makes a contribution to national survival. Nursery sheepdog trials, however, do marry the practical with the competitive – and the social. They have become established features of north country winters, where the season's young entries and older non-winners are put through their paces on cold hillsides not far from the scene of their normal work.

A nursery trial is not for the comfort-loving, or for Shakespeare's men who 'come to take their ease'. Its only windbreak is the car window, its sole grandstand the arc of vehicles lining hedge or stone wall. The worse the weather, the greater the need for shepherding skills, so fog is the only hazard likely to stop a trial. Dark sheep, black-marked dogs, dull sky over sombre, distant hills and grey stone walls provide the likeliest colour combination.

Even in the heaviest thunderstorm the shepherd still takes his stance. One story is told of a septuagenarian handler who succeeded with his round because the sheep ran into the pen for shelter from the downpour. Strong winds, snow or flood make conditions difficult, but they do on the hills as well, and the whole point of a trial is to put day-to-day working conditions on a competitive basis.

To do this, a small number of sheep are let out at the far end of the field, a quarter to half a mile distant from the handler at his stake. He sets his dog away on the left hand or the right, according to the lie of the land and, perhaps, the aptitude of the particular animal. The collie should describe a wide arc and come quietly behind its little flock, 'lifting' them in a firm but quiet manner and fetching them between two hurdles in as straight a line as possible practice for a budding international winner.

Sheep and dog then take a triangular course

through two more sets of hurdles, and return. The flock is confronted with a small pen with a gate attached into which they must be guided, and on release one sheep is split from the rest, or the flock halved.

It is simple to describe. To carry out the succession of manœuvres calls for aptitude and obedience, the former inherited from generations of selective breeding, the reaction to commands patiently being instilled from an early age.

Until the pup begins to 'run', little can be attempted. 'Running', in sheepmen's language, means rounding up almost anything that moves, including, and especially, any farmyard hens and ducks. Poultry seldom have the freedom of the stackyard these days, so perform less frequently that very useful if unsought distinction of providing practice for a budding international winner.

Walking under command at heel and prompt reaction to the 'Lie down' signal or whistle are among the trainee's first lessons. Dogs handled by top trainers differ from the more lax members of their breed: they 'clap' immediately the single long blast – the universal 'Stop' whistle – rends the air: they do not crawl on to the next bit of cover or avoid a wet place – they stop there and then. Such obedience prevents loss of points at a trial and, more practically, is an insurance against undue harrying of a flock heavy because they are in lamb.

Working in a small flock in a field corner, the dog moves to its left or right, and is given the appropriate direction signal. Eventually this is associated with the action, which becomes instant reaction to an apparently meaningless set of whistles. From whistles meaning Stop, Come, Heel, move to right or left, or straight ahead to its sheep, a flock is manœuvred by the dog into almost any position.

Between the ages of a few months and two years a pup is learning these lessons. If its owner is trial-minded and the youngster shows promise, they go to the nearest nurseries, pay the small entry fee, and await their turn.

The newcomer is noted by men whose lives revolve round sheep and dogs. Its back-breeding is soon ascertained; a grandson of Wiston Cap, perhaps, who after winning the International Sheep Dog Society's Supreme Championship at two years old has sired over 1 000 pups: or sired by a more recent winner, John Murray's Glen, or going back to McKnight's Gael. Does it attempt to rush its sheep, or turn round timidly when faced with a stamping Blackface ewe with large round horns? Is reaction to direction whistles instantaneous? Was the easy penning due to good, amenable sheep or correct amount of 'eye' and movement?

Judges' points are deducted, the kitty shared among the winners, and dogs and men return to another week's work on the hills. They have confidence in their vocation, in the knowledge that they are producing meat and wool this year and will be next year, the kind of tangible results which the conifer planters, who have taken over so much sound hill land, cannot achieve in 50 years.

Spectators have had a day in the open air and the company of men to whom their work is the most interesting thing in their lives. And among that bunch of rather raw collies, one may some day receive the applause of a large crowd, with a winning run to gain the Supreme.

EDWARD HART *The Times*

Comprehension and interpretation – discuss or write answers

1 What is the difference between nursery sheepdog trials and most of our other national sports?
2 In what part of Britain and at what time of year are these trials held?
3 What sort of weather can one expect on many of these occasions?
4 What is the whole point of these trials?
5 What is another name for a sheepdog?
6 What is the final objective of the handler and his dog at the trial?
7 Mention some of the lessons a sheepdog has to learn in training.
8 What gives the shepherds a confidence and knowledge that conifer planters cannot achieve in 50 years?

The poet speaks

The sportsman

Nature he loves, and next to Nature – death.
When he deprives some creature of its breath
The man is happy in his joyless fashion;
For sport to him's a stern compulsive passion,
And in its service he devotes his leisure
Proving how grimly men can take their pleasure.

In better days, when maps were red, not Red,
He courted lions till those lions were dead;
Conducted, with a shrewd appraising eye,
Brisk love affair with hippopotami;
And when he hunted tigers with a rajah
The ones he bagged were usually the larger.

Now, with the cost of living to enforce it,
Extermination is confined to Dorset.
He can't indulge his old romantic habits
And must content himself with potting rabbits –
Or pheasants, at a friend's estate near Sherborne,
So stuffed with corn as to be scarcely airborne.

But in his dreams voluptuous rhinos swim
And tigers roar their enormous love for him,
While he, with tenderly-selected slugs,
Converts them all to trophies or to rugs . . .
To me the situation is ironic:
Thank God my love of Nature is platonic!

CLIVE SANSOM *Dorset Village* (born 1912)

For discussion

How does this sportsman differ from those other sportsmen and women whose games have been mentioned in Unit 4? Would all-in wrestlers enjoy being a sportsman of the kind referred to by Clive Sansom? What is the poet's view of people who deprive some creature of its breath?
Must a sport be competitive and organised to be enjoyable? Justify your answer.
What is the point of 'blood sports'?

The language of poetry

To hear the lark begin his flight,
And, singing, startle the dull night,
From his watch-tower in the skies,
Till the dappled dawn doth rise; . . .
While the cock, with lively din,
Scatters the rear of darkness thin;
And to the stack or the barn door,
Stoutly struts his dames before.
Oft listening how the hounds and horn
Cheerly rouse the slumbering morn
From the side of some hoar hill,
Through the high wood echoing shrill.
Sometimes walking, not unseen,
By hedgerow elms, on hillocks green,
Right against the eastern gate
When the great sun begins his state,
Robed in flames and amber light,
The clouds in thousand liveries dight,
While the ploughman, near at hand,
Whistles o'er the furrowed land,
And the milkmaid singeth blithe,
And the mower whets his scythe,
And every shepherd tells his tale
Under the hawthorn in the dale.

JOHN MILTON (1608–1674)

For discussion

1 Study and consider the use and sound of these words and expressions from Milton's poem:
    dappled dawn   stoutly struts   hounds and horn
2 Why does the cock lead the hens to the stack or the barn door?
3 What does Milton mean by *gate* in line 15?
4 *Dight* in line 18 means clad or adorned. Explain the word *liveries* in this line.
5 *Tell* in line 23 means count. What is the shepherd doing?
6 How does a mower *whet his scythe*?
7 What is *furrowed land*?
8 What is a dale?

To take you further

Read this poem aloud and add some sound effects of your own choosing. You might record your work on tape and play it back to discuss the success or failure of your efforts.

The storm

Against the stone breakwater,
Only an ominous lapping,
While the wind whines overhead,
Coming down from the mountain,
Whistling between the arbours, the winding
    terraces;
A thin whine of wires, a rattling and flapping of
    leaves,
And the small streetlamp swinging and slamming
    against the lamp-pole.
Where have the people gone?
There is one light on the mountain.
Along the sea-wall a steady sloshing of the swell,
The waves not yet high, but even,
Coming closer and closer upon each other;
A fine fume of rain driving in from the sea,
Riddling the sand, like a wide spray of buckshot,
The wind from the sea and the wind from the
    mountain contending,
Flicking the foam from the whitecaps straight
    upwards into the darkness.
A time to go home!
And a child's dirty shift billows upward out of an
    alley;
A cat runs from the wind as we do,
Between the whitening trees, up Santa Lucia
Where the heavy door unlocks
And our breath comes more easy.
Then a crack of thunder, and the black rain runs
    over us, over
The flat-roofed houses, coming down in gusts,
    beating
The walls, the slatted windows, driving
The last watcher indoors, moving the cardplayers
    closer
To their cards, their Lachryma Christi.

We creep to our bed and its straw mattress.
We wait, we listen.
The storm lulls off, then redoubles,
Bending the trees halfway down to the ground,
Shaking loose the last wizened oranges in the
    orchard,
Flattening the limber carnations.
A spider eases himself down from a swaying light
    bulb,
Running over the coverlet, down under the iron
    bedstead.
The bulb goes on and off, weakly.
Water roars in the cistern.
We lie closer on the gritty pillow,
Breathing heavily, hoping –
For the great last leap of the wave over the
    breakwater,
The flat boom on the beach of the towering sea-
    swell,
The sudden shudder as the jutting sea-cliff
    collapses
And the hurricane drives the dead straw into the
    living pine-tree.

            THEODORE ROETHKE (1908–1963)

Write what you think about the use of words in this poem, but discuss it in groups first.

Poetry for pleasure – library work

Find and read: *Second glance at a Jaguar* by TED
    HUGHES (from *Wodwo*) Faber
and: *The Arrival of the Bee Box* by SYLVIA PLATH
(from *Ariel*) Faber

For your information

Purcell composed a delightful duet, *Let Us Wander*, using the last six lines of the poem by John Milton. (The words of the first two lines are by Dryden and Harrod.) You can hear a recording of this on HMV HLM 7002 in a recital by Isobel Baillie and Kathleen Ferrier.

Study these two pictures

Describe Spencer's picture after you have found out about swan upping, and explain why the swans' wings are bound. What kind of paints has Spencer used? Has Marc Chagall used the same paints? Now look at *The poet reclining* and describe what you think the artist is telling you about a poet's thoughts and ideas. Or is he just showing a 'pretty picture'?

Visual discussions

See if you can obtain some of the following slides and records and then organise group discussions. Either report or tape your discussions for the rest of the class to consider. (Have the materials available to show the others when you make your report.)
Slides – with National Gallery, London numbers in brackets:
Sea Battle at Sunset – Turner (508)
Sun Rising through Vapour – Turner (479)
The Flood – Monet (6278)
Two Watermills – Ruisdael (986)
Venice – van de Velde (876)
The Fighting Temeraire – Turner (524)

Discography
Radio Ballad: Singing the Fishing by Ewan MacColl and Charles Parker.
Sea and Water – sound effects, BBC Enterprises, Villiers House, Haven Green, London W5 2PA.
Sea Symphony: Vaughan Williams
Fire bird Suite: Stravinsky
Orpheus: Liszt
Rhapsody in Blue: Gershwin

Explain the value of these recordings and try to relate them to some of the writing and pictures you have met in this unit or in previous units in this book.

The country code

- Leave no litter – take it home
- Guard against all risk of fire
- Fasten all gates
- Safeguard water supplies
- Go carefully on country roads
- Avoid damaging fences, hedges and wells
- Keep dogs under proper control
- Keep to paths across farm land
- Respect the life of the countryside
- Protect wild life, wild plants and trees

Reading for pleasure

The earth in fertile wools is spread with yellow and blue carpets of primroses, violets, and hyacinths, over which the birch-trees, like stooping nymphs, hang with their thickening hair. Lilies-of-the-valley, stocks, columbines, ladysmocks, and the intensely red peony which seems to anticipate the full glow of summertime, all come out to wait upon the season, like fairies from their subterranean palaces.

LEIGH HUNT (1784–1859)

The sunny slow lulling afternoon yawns and moons through the dozy town. The sea lolls, laps and idles in, with fishes sleeping in its lap. The meadows still as Sunday, the shut-eye tasselled bulls, the coat-and-daisy dingles, nap happy and lazy. The dumb duck-ponds snooze. Clouds sag and pillow on Llaregub Hill. Pigs grunt in a wet-wallow bath, and smile as they snort and dream.

DYLAN THOMAS *Under Milkwood* (1914–1953)

The sea is flecked with bars of grey,
The dull dead wind is out of tune,
And like a withered leaf the moon
Is blown across the stormy bay.

Etched clear upon the pallid sand
The black boat lies: a sailor boy
Clambers aboard in careless joy
With laughing face and gleaming hand.

And overhead the curlews cry,
Where through the dusky upland grass
The young brown-throated reapers pass,
Like silhouettes against the sky.

OSCAR WILDE (1854–1900)

Creative writing

Either Write a short description of a crowded seaside scene, then contrast it with the same beach late at night, deserted and silent in the moonlight; *Or* contrast a busy supermarket in daytime with the same scene at night.

For discussion

1 Consider the somewhat idealized style of the Leigh Hunt passage (notice the comparisons – 'like stooping nymphs', etc. – and the early Victorian *romantic tone*); compare it with Dylan Thomas's more sophisticated, modern treatment (notice his use of metaphor 'the afternoon yawns and moons', etc. –). But is he less *sentimental*?

2 Could you find examples of paintings to show a similar sort of contrast between Victorian and modern pictures? Try D G Rossetti compared with John Bratby. What about sculpture in this context? (There may be local examples and contrasts of paintings and sculptures.)

Reading for pleasure

1 *Water picture*

In the pond in the park
all things are doubled:
Long buildings hang and
wriggle gently. Chimneys
are bent legs bouncing
on clouds below. A flag
wags like a fish-hook
down there in the sky.

The arched stone bridge
is an eye, with underlid
in the water. In its lens
dip crinkled heads with hats
that don't fall off. Dogs go by,
barking on their backs . . .
MAY SWENSON *To Mix with Time*

Treetops deploy a haze of
cherry bloom for roots,
where birds coast belly-up
in the glass bowl of a hill . . .

A swan, with twin necks
forming the figure three,
steers between two dimpled
towers doubled. Fondly,
hissing, she hisses herself,
and all the scene is troubled:
water-windows splinter,
tree-limbs tangle, the bridge
folds like a fan.

2 *My wish*

And I wish that all times were April and May,
and every month renew all fruits again, and every
day fleur-de-lis and gillyflower and violets and roses
wherever one goes, and woods in leaf and meadows
green,
and every lover should have his lass, and they to
love each other with a sure heart and true, and to
everyone his pleasure and a gay heart.

Anon (student, thirteenth century) Paris

3 *Aim high!*

Who shoots at the midday sun, though he shall be
sure
he shall never hit the mark, yet as sure he is, he
shall shoot higher than who aims at a bush.

SIR PHILIP SIDNEY (1554–1586)

Man and nature

Read this story, then answer the questions which follow:

There was once a town where all life seemed to live in harmony with its surroundings. The town lay in the midst of a checkerboard of prosperous farms, with fields of grain and hillsides of orchards where, in spring, white clouds of bloom drifted above the green fields. In autumn, oak and maple and birch set up a blaze of colour that flamed and flickered across a backdrop of pines. Then foxes barked in the hills and deer silently crossed the fields, half hidden in the mists of the autumn mornings.

Along the roads, laurel, viburnum and alder, great ferns and wildflowers delighted the traveller's eye through much of the year. Even in winter the roadsides were places of beauty, where countless birds came to feed on the berries and on the seed heads of the dried weeds riding above the snow. The countryside was, in fact, famous for the abundance and variety of its bird life, and when the flood of migrants was pouring through in spring and autumn people travelled from great distances to observe them. Others came to fish the streams, which flowed clear and cold out of the hills and contained shady pools where trout lay. So it had been from the days many years ago when the first settlers raised their homes, sank their wells, and built their barns.

Then a strange blight crept over the area and everything began to change. Some evil spell had settled on the community: mysterious maladies swept the flocks of chickens; the cattle and sheep sickened and died. Everywhere was a shadow of death. The farmers spoke of much illness among their families. In the town the doctors had become more and more puzzled by new kinds of sickness appearing among their patients. There had been several sudden and unexplained deaths, not only among adults but even among children, who would be stricken suddenly while at play and die within a few hours.

There was a strange stillness. The birds, for example – where had they gone? Many people spoke of them, puzzled and disturbed. The feeding stations in the backyards were deserted. The few birds seen anywhere were moribund; they trembled violently and could not fly. It was a spring without voices. On the mornings that had once throbbed with the dawn chorus of robins, catbirds, doves, jays, wrens, and scores of other birds' voices there was now no sound; only silence lay over the fields and woods and marsh.

On the farms the hens brooded, but no chicks hatched. The farmers complained that they were unable to raise any pigs – the litters were small and the young survived only a few days. The apple trees were coming into bloom but no bees droned among the blossoms, so there was no pollination and there would be no fruit.

The roadsides, once so attractive, were now lined with browned and withered vegetation as though swept by fire. These, too, were silent, deserted by all living things. Even the streams were now lifeless. Anglers no longer visited them, for all the fish had died.

No witchcraft, no enemy action had silenced the rebirth of new life in this stricken world. The people had done it themselves.

RACHEL CARSON *Silent Spring* (1907–1964)

Reading for meaning

1 The above is not a true story. It is fiction, but fiction designed to point a moral – what may be called a *parable*. Read it again and then discuss in what ways it is true today of some of the things that are happening to our countryside in Britain. (Rachel Carson was referring to America in her parable above.)

2 List the present-day man-made enemies of nature, e.g. transport, factories, fuel, with details of their effect on the countryside.
3 Why are some animals, birds and butterflies in danger of becoming extinct?

Creative writing

Write a short piece describing the scene before and after a block of ugly luxury flats has replaced a row of charming houses.

Sing-song

Chant the following description of present-day farming by John Betjeman – the tune as for the hymn *We plough the fields and scatter* (number 383). If you prefer read it aloud – *vigorously*! Then discuss whether it is a fair description of farmers' work and attitudes today? (Refer to page 69 for the farmers' retort.)

> We spray the fields and scatter
>   The poison on the ground
> So that no wicked wild flowers
>   Upon our farms are found.
> We like whatever helps us
>   To line our purse with pence;
> The twenty-four hour broiler house
>   And sweet electric fence.
>
> All concrete sheds around us
>   And Jaguars in the yard
> The tele lounge and deep-freeze
>   Are ours for working hard.
> We fire the fields for harvest
>   The hedges swell the flame,
> The oak trees and the cottages
>   From which our fathers came.
>
> We give no compensation,
>   The earth is ours today
> And if we lost on arable,
>   Then bungalows will pay.
>
> All concrete yards . . . etc.

The artist speaks

Old man figuring by Paul Klee (1879–1940)

Dead bird by Albrecht Dürer. This was painted in 1512.

Composition

Write a story based on the picture of *Spaghetti junction* on page 56.

Visual awareness

Write down two sentences about Klee's *Old man figuring* and two about Dürer's *Dead bird*. Then discuss these illustrations.

A chance to act

The visitor – a play for two people.

This is a three minute play. Either mime the play or make up your own words. You can write your script either before or after you make up the words.

  Divide into groups of two and choose which plan of action you like best for the two people in your play: the Old Lady and the Visitor.

PLAN OF ACTION
(a) The Old Lady is:
  – in bed and asleep
  – lying on a rug in the garden
  – looking at TV
  – eating breakfast
  – knitting
  – writing a letter

(b) The Visitor enters and
  – shouts at the sleeping old lady
  – places a box of chocolates on the rug beside her
  – trips over her
  – switches off the TV
  – pours out a cup of tea
  – offers to lend her a stamp

(c) Who is the Visitor?
  – the doctor
  – an old friend
  – the postman
  – a burglar
  – a grandchild
  – a policeman

(d) The Old Lady is
  – pleased
  – angry
  – pretending to be blind
  – worried
  – afraid
  – helpful
  – irritable

Mime or act with your own words any pairing of the sections above.

Tailpieces

1 To every thing there is a season, and a time to every purpose under the heaven: a time to be born, and a time to die; a time to plant, and a time to pluck up that which is planted; a time to kill, and a time to heal; a time to break down, and a time to build up; a time to weep, and a time to laugh; a time to mourn, and a time to dance; a time to cast away stones, and a time to gather stones together; a time to embrace, and a time to refrain from embracing; a time to seek, and a time to lose; a time to keep, and a time to cast away; a time to rend, and a time to sew; a time to keep silence, and a time to speak; a time to love, and a time to hate; a time for war, and a time for peace.

ECCLESIASTES Chapter 3

2 *The Brutes*

I think I could turn and live with animals, they
   are so placid and self-contain'd;
I stand and look at them sometimes half the day
   long.
They do not sweat and whine about their
   condition;
They do not lie awake in the dark and weep for
   their sins; . . .
Not one is dissatisfied – not one is demented with
   the mania of owning things; . . .
Not one is respectable or industrious over the
   whole earth.

WALT WHITMAN

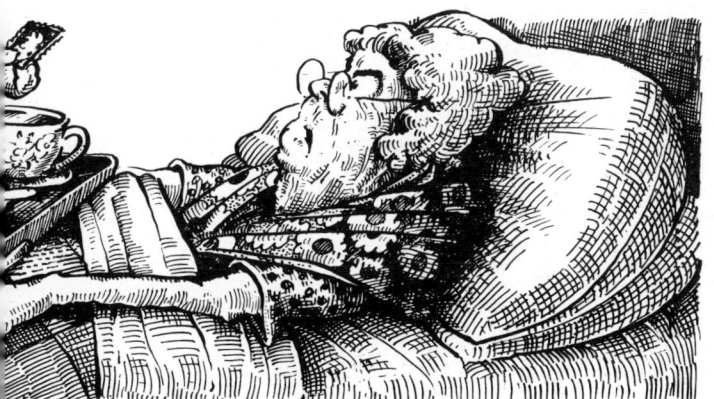

3 *Throwing a tree: New Forest*

The two executioners stalk along over the
   knolls,
Bearing two axes with heavy heads shining
   and wide,
And a long limp two-handled saw toothed for
   cutting great boles
And so they approach the proud tree that bears
   the death-mark on its side.

Jackets doffed they swing axes and chop away
   just above ground,
And the chips fly about and lie white on the
   moss and fallen leaves;
Till a broad deep gash in the bark is hewn all
   the way round,
And one of them tries to hook upward a rope,
   which at last he achieves.

The saw then begins, till the top of the tall
   giant shivers:
The shivers are seen to grow greater each cut
   than before:
They edge out the saw, tug the rope; but the
   tree only quivers,
And kneeling and sawing again, they step back
   to try pulling once more.

Then, lastly, the living mast sways, further
   sway: with a shout
Job and Ike rush aside. Reached the end of its
   long staying powers
The tree crashes downward: it shakes all its
   neighbours throughout
And two hundred years' steady growth has been
   ended in less than two hours.

THOMAS HARDY (1840–1928)

For discussion

Point out two or three words in the first verse
which strike you as particularly expressive.
Describe briefly in your own words what happens
before the actual sawing begins.
What are the poet's feelings about throwing a tree?

Audio-visual aids

Films. 16mm Available from National Audio-Visual Aids Library, Paxton Place, Gipsy Road, London SE27 9SR.

Animals in Spring 614 D18
Sound film in colour, 11 mins with teachers' notes.
Encyclopaedia Britannica distributed by Rank.
This film considers the activities of animals while caring for the young born in Spring: preparing home-gathering food and feeding offspring – protecting the young. Included are birds, squirrels, foxes, rabbits, frogs, fish and insects.

Animals in Summer 614 D15
As above searching for food for winter, storing food, watching over the young until independent, etc.

Animals in Autumn 614 D17
As above. Animals include deer, foxes, rabbits, squirrels, birds and insects. Typical autumn activities and preparing for migration and hibernation.

Farm animals. Sound Film in black and white with Teachers' notes. 617 A6
A farmer on a typical farm going through the day caring for animals – a new born calf and colt, young pigs and lambs, a goat and kids and sheep. Natural sounds are included.

Man through his Art – Man and Animal
16 slides in colour, 4 in black and white with teachers' notes.
Unesco distributed by Educational Productions Ltd., East Ardsley, Wakefield, Yorks.
Panta Rhei Sound film in black and white. 20 mins. An abstract picture depicting rhythm in nature.
Royal Netherlands Embassy distributed by National Audio Visual Aids Paxton Place, Gipsy Road, London SE27 9SS.
The Open Window 18 mins sound film in colour.
A journey through the countryside of five countries as great painters have seen it during five centuries of the development of landscape painting.

The farmers' retort (see page 65)

So make us farmers humble,
   Take all our perks away,
Convert the rippling cornfield
   And sweet green clover ley
To wilderness of ragwort,
   Of couch and scrub and gorse.
God, make the rabbits flourish,
   Turn tractor into horse.

Chorus:

Make concrete yards to crumble,
   Give Jags to those who seek
To live life as it should be:
   The townsman's four-day week.

C T JESSEL

Books and poems

Camping and Caravans by JOHN SHARP Macdonald
Introduction to Nature (Insects, Fishes, Birds, etc.) by
    MAURICE BURTON Macdonald
Are Animals Different? by DR VESELOVSKY Methuen
Sea Angling for Beginners by ALAN YOUNG Pan
Canal Fishing by KENNETH SEAMAN Pan
Boat Fishing by TREVOR HOUSBY Pan
SOS Save the Earth published by Collins
Project Earth: An Action Guide by GRAHAM SEARLE
Woolfe
New Naturalist Series published by Collins
Everyman's Nature Reserve: Ideas for Action David and
    Charles
For these poems consult popular anthologies. Look
under author entry or ask a librarian.
Death of a Naturalist SEAMUS HEANEY
Postscript W H AUDEN
Some thoughts on the Common Toad GEORGE ORWELL
Man Carrying Bale by HAROLD MONROE
The Herd Boy by LU YU (translated by Arthur Waley)
Mouse's Nest by JOHN CLARE
An August Midnight by THOMAS HARDY
Pike by TED HUGHES
Wild Swans at Coole by W B YEATS
Orpheus by TED HUGHES

Discography

The Wasps Overture by Vaughan Williams (1872–
1958)
The Year's Journey Record (RED 135 M) from BBC
Records London SE19 1UE.

The last word

Aii Aii (An Eskimo Song)

I think over again my small adventures
When with the wind I drifted in my Kayak
And thought I was in danger
My fears
Those small ones that seemed so big
For all the vital things
I had to get and to reach
And yet there is only one great thing
The only thing
To live to see the great day that dawns
And the light that fills the world.
          Trs by Tegoodligak, South Baffin Island

Filmstrip in colour
Eskimo Sculpture. Sound Services Ltd., Kingston
Road, London SW19 3NR.

Useful addresses

Forestry Commission
25 Savile Row, London W1X 2AY.

Countryside Commission
1 Cambridge Gate, London NW1 4JY.

The Nature Conservancy
19 Belgrave Square, London SW1X 8PY.

The Council for the Protection of Rural England
4 Hobart Place, London SW1W 0HY.

7. Group B folder work

Research projects

1 Choose six of the following. Make notes or tapes and report your findings in the form of an illustrated notebook and a poster with pictures and/or diagrams.
Why moles are useful
How fishes breathe
Why the legs and feet of birds vary so much in shape and length
Which insects are useful and which harmful
How the earth worm is the gardener's best friend
How many classes of bee live in one hive and the job each performs
Why a spider is not an insect
What sponges are
The difference between a smolt and a grilse
How dew ponds are formed
Why sound travels so easily over water
Why the sun looks red when it is near the horizon
Why some stars that have already disappeared are still visible

2 *Apples and orchards*
If you live in Kent or Worcestershire you will know that originally most cultivated apples were wild crab apples. Apples and orchards can form a fascinating project wherever you live. Here are a few guidelines for you to develop. Use charts, maps, pictures and photographs. Find out the origin of Cox's Orange Pippins. What are the advantages of the Kent 'bush' orchards?

Where do apples go after picking?
What is a 'grading station'?
Where do apples go to from the grading stations?
How and from where do apples reach your local shop?
From which countries do foreign apples come?
What routes do they take to England?
What sort of soil is best for apple orchards?
What weather is good, what bad for orchards?
How do fruit farmers protect trees from pests?
Describe and name the birds that can be heard singing in orchards.
Refer to Band 2 of *Year's Journey Record* (RED 135 M) from BBC Records, London S.E.97. (for bird songs)

3 *Camping*
Compile a useful guide with details and advice for beginners.

4 *Pigeons*
If you live in a town or city you could make a survey of the pigeon problem by reporting on their nesting places and habits and by suggesting ways of keeping them out.
Racing pigeons could form the subject of your project if you prefer.

5 *Noise*
Report on road traffic and aircraft noise. Then go on to transistors and any other nuisances, including late night parties!

Random information which may be useful
Write to Watch Club, 32 Trumpington Road, Cambridge, for details of their activities and projects.

The map labels (from the illustration):

National Parks
Areas considered as future National Parks
Forest Parks

OUTER HEBRIDES
INNER HEBRIDES
WESTERN HIGHLANDS
SCOTLAND
Glenmore (Cairngorms)
Ben Nevis
Argyll
Ben Lomond
Edinburgh
SOUTHERN UPLANDS
Border
Glen Trool
GALLOWAY
Northumberland (Cheviots)
Isle of Man
Lake District
Yorkshire Dales
North York Moors
NORTH SEA
IRISH SEA
Blackpool
Manchester
Anglesey
Snowdonia
Peak District (Derbyshire Dales)
Skegness
The Wash
Cambrian
MIDLANDS
Black Country
Norfolk Broads
EAST ANGLIA
WALES
ENGLAND
R. Severn
Pembroke Coast
Brecon Beacons
Black Mts.
Forest of Dean
Glamorgan
Cotswolds
Chilterns
LONDON
Southend
Gower Peninsula
R. Thames
SOMERSET
KENT
Exmoor
New Forest
DEVON
Rye
Dartmoor
Brighton
CORNWALL
Isle of Wight
Scilly Is.
ENGLISH CHANNEL

National parks

Choose one of the areas marked on this map which shows the National Parks in Britain.

Then write a survey of the area you choose under the most appropriate of the following headings.

Illustrate with sketch maps and photographs if you wish.

How to get there
How to get around
 (transport services)
Where to stay
(consult YHA Handbook)
Camping and Caravan sites
Maps – give Ordnance Survey
 sheet numbers
What to read
 (e.g. Wordsworth might
 be mentioned by those
 who choose the Lake
 District)
Walking – describe the terrain
Climbing
 and mountaineering
Boating
Swimming (lakes, etc.)
Fishing
Weather
Wildlife
Useful addresses
Nature trails (if any)
Places of historical and other
 interest – Abbeys, walls, etc.
Pony Trekking
Caves

8. On the move – in Britain

A holiday morning

There was no need, that holiday morning, for the sluggardly boys to be shouted down to breakfast; out of their jumbled beds they tumbled, scrambled into their rumpled clothes; quickly at the bathroom basic they catlicked their hands and faces, but never forgot to run the water loud and long as though they washed like colliers; in front of the cracked looking-glass bordered with cigarette-cards, in their treasure-trove bedrooms, they whisked a gap-tooth comb through their surly hair, and with shining cheeks and noses and tidemarked necks, they took the stairs three at a time.

But for all their scramble and scamper, clamour on the landing, catlick and toothbrush flick, hair-whisk and stair-jump, their sisters were always there before them. Up with the lady lark, they had prinked and fizzed and hot-ironed; and smug in their blossoming dresses, ribboned for the sun, in gym-shoes white as the blanco'd snow, neat and silly with doilies and tomatoes they helped in the higgledy kitchen. They were calm; they were virtuous; they had washed their necks, they did not romp, or fidget; and only the smallest sister put out her tongue at the noisy boys.

And the woman who lived next door came into the kitchen and said that her mother, an ancient uncertain body who wore a hat with cherries, was having 'one of her days' and had insisted, that very holiday morning, on carrying all the way to the tram-stop a photograph album and the cut-glass fruit-bowl from the front room.

This was the morning when father, mending one hole in the thermos-flask, made three; when the sun declared war on the butter, and the butter ran; when dogs, with all the sweet-binned backyards to wag and sniff and bicker in, chased their tails in the jostling kitchen, worried sandshoes, snapped at flies, writhed between legs, scratched among towels, sat smiling on hampers.

DYLAN THOMAS (1914–1953)

Comprehension and deduction

1 Why was there no need for the boys *to be shouted down to breakfast* on this occasion?
2 What proof is there that the boys' bedrooms were not particularly tidy?
3 Why did the boys *run the water loud and long*?
4 Why did they *take the stairs three at a time*?
5 For what reasons were their sisters downstairs before them?
6 What single piece of evidence suggests that the girls had taken more care than the boys in getting ready?
7 How do we know that most of the sisters were better behaved than their brothers?
8 What proof is there that this was going to be a hot day?
9 Make a list of things that happened which may well have made the family late in setting off.
10 How do you know that the family were going to the seaside?

Interpretation and criticism

1 On what mornings would the boys really be *sluggardly*?
2 What does the word *jumbled* suggest about the state of their beds?
3 What does the word *rumpled* suggest about their clothes?
4 Which word in the first paragraph effectively suggests that the boys' washes were as hasty as could be?

5 Why would colliers *run the water loud and long*?
6 Typical of Dylan Thomas is his ability to suggest so much in a single word or pair of words. Describe the probable appearance of a *treasure-trove* bedroom.
7 Which words in paragraph 2 suggest the careless speed of the boys' preparations?
8 What does the word *higgledy* suggest about the probable appearance of the kitchen whilst everyone was preparing to go out?
9 Why did the boys romp and fidget, but not the girls?
10 Why were the backyards *sweet-binned* – as far as the dogs were concerned?
11 Why was the kitchen described as *jostling*?

Comment and discussion

1 A great deal of Dylan Thomas's prose and poetry can be enjoyed and appreciated more when read aloud. Read the above passage aloud and consider whether your enjoyment grows as a result. Explain why reading aloud reveals more of the atmosphere of 'that holiday morning' to you.
2 Try to decide exactly what it is about Dylan Thomas's manner of writing that makes this passage so original in style and detail.
3 How does this passage show that comedy can be found in very ordinary settings? Discuss television programmes which make use of such ordinary settings for. what is known as 'situation comedy'.
4 Talk or write about holiday preparations which had their hectic moments in your home.

Over the sea to Skye

We were quite used to Youth Hostelling in Britain on foot and on bicycles, but last summer we had a holiday *de luxe*.

We chose Skye when my wife's parents suggested it and gave us the return fare from London to Perth as a twenty-first birthday present for my wife. We were able to borrow my father's car and take it with us on the train as far as Perth.

In fact, everything combined to make it possible for us to travel further afield by car instead of on foot or by bicycle. Furthermore, we knew it was the last chance of a real walking holiday together for some years as our first baby was due at Christmas. After that, it would be buckets and spades instead of bicycles and mountains!

So we put the car on the train at King's Cross and slept our way to Perth. I will not bore you with minute details of scenery, with tedious descriptions of routes, but in case you ever get the chance to make this enchanting trip, let me give a brief outline. From Perth make for Inverness along the A82, then turn west for one of the loveliest roads to the isles and take the A832 to Loch Carron. From there visit Sheildaig and walk across to have a look at Loch Torridon.

We did this and then crossed by ferry to Skye at Kyle of Lochalsh and drove straight to Glen Brittle where we camped for a week. There is a magnificent Youth Hostel there and we met many other walkers and many expert climbers. Of course, we walked over the Cuillins to Loch Coruisk and you had better read the guide books for a description of the scenery there – what they say is true. The expected clichés about a wonderful experience, about the exhilaration, the hazards, the companionship are all true, too.

Even the walk is hard going. For climbers on the Cuillins it is really tough. If the clouds come down, and they do so with a terrible suddenness, you may freeze to death if you stay still. If you try to move you may fall hundreds of feet to your death.

We had perfect weather in Skye: 'unnatural' the locals called it. We also saw something of the other

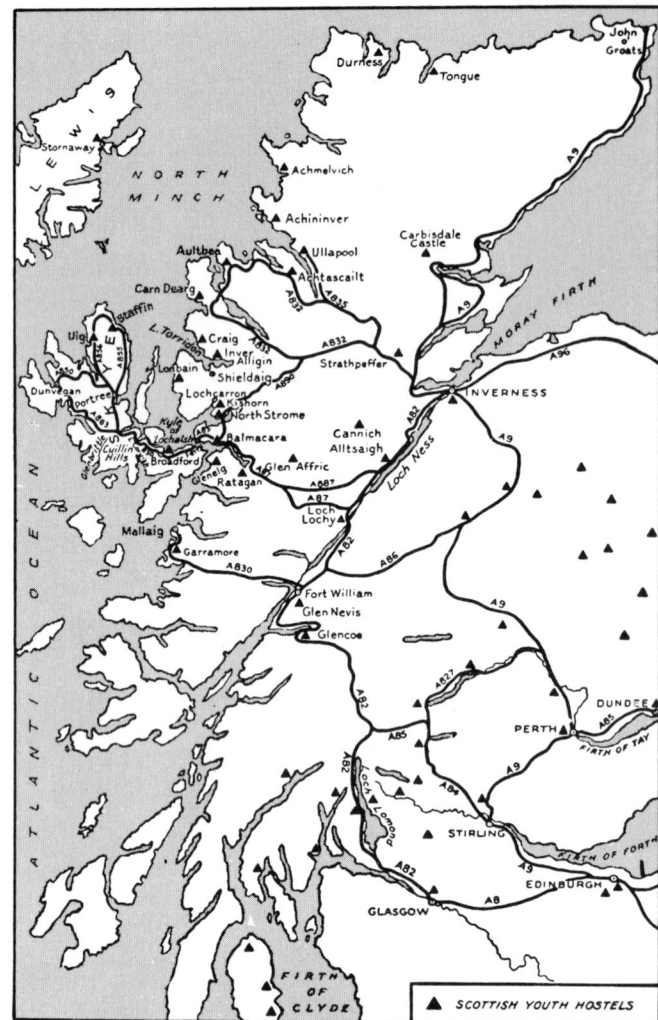

isles, and on the way back to Perth via Mallaig (A830) we twice stopped a night at a Youth Hostel. It was one of those holidays called *unforgettable*.

We recorded it all with my camera, in colour. When our children are old enough (we hope to have four of them) we must take them to Glen Brittle. But before that we must introduce them to Youth Hostelling in England. Once they've had a taste of this they'll soon adventure further afield to the Continent and to Scotland. I'm sure they'll be tough enough, maybe one of them will conquer the Cuillins and *then* tackle the Himalayas!

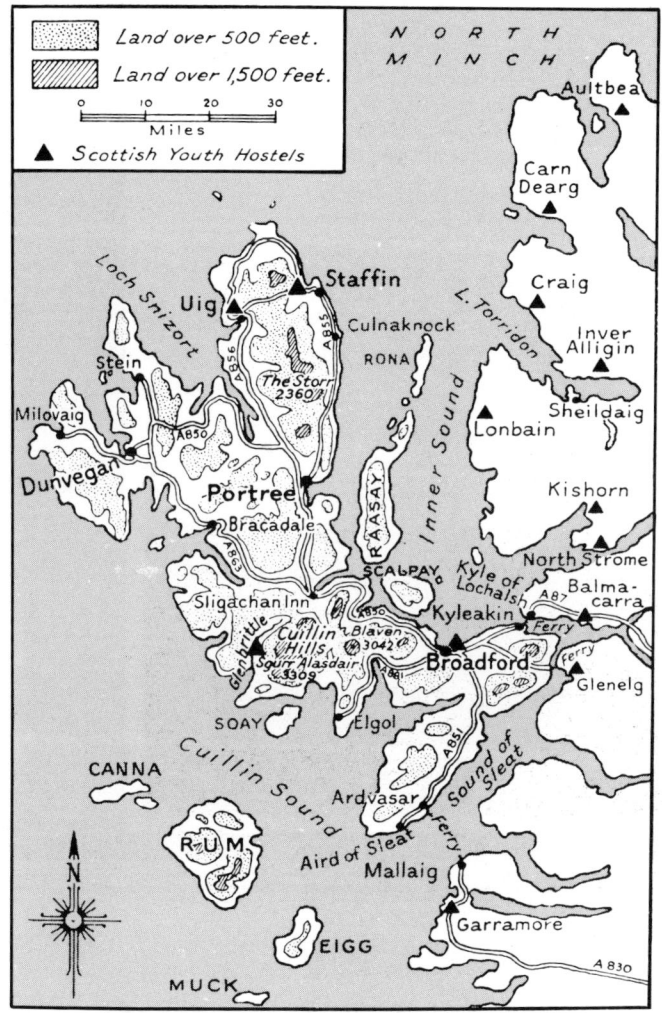

Map legend:

Land over 500 feet.
Land over 1,500 feet.

0   10   20   30
Miles

▲ Scottish Youth Hostels

NORTH MINCH

Aultbea ▲
Carn Dearg ▲
Craig ▲
L. Torridon
Inver Alligin ▲
RONA
Sheildaig ▲
Lonbain ▲
Kishorn ▲
North Strome ▲
Balma-carra
Kyle of Lochalsh
Glenelg
Sound of Sleat

Loch Snizort
Uig ▲
Staffin ▲
Culnaknock
Stein
The Storr 2360
Milovaig
A850
Dunvegan
Portree ▲
Bracadale
RAASAY
Inner Sound
SCALPAY
Sligachan Inn
Kyleakin
Ferry
Cuillin Hills Blaven 3042
Sgurr Alasdair 3309
Broadford ▲
SOAY
Elgol
CANNA
Cuillin Sound
Ardvasar
RUM
Aird of Sleat
Mallaig
Garramore
EIGG
MUCK
A830
N

Comprehension and interpretation

1 What two factors made it possible for the writer and his wife to have a holiday *de luxe* last summer?
2 Why was it their last chance of a real walking holiday for some years?
3 Which part of the journey was made by train?
4 In what country was this holiday spent?
5 What range of hills lies between Glen Brittle and Loch Coruisk?
6 What is a cliché? Give an example.

7 Follow the route outlined on these maps provided.
8 Explain the meaning of:
   exhilaration   hazard   de luxe   the Continent
9 What may happen if the clouds envelop you at 3 000 feet?
10 What sort of summer weather would you usually expect in the Cuillins?
11 What particular adjective does the writer use to describe this holiday?
12 In what way can they refresh the child's eye about this trip in future years?
13 How many children do they hope to have?
14 Through what organisation is this sort of holiday available to able-bodied young people?
15 Explain *initiative*.
16 What famous mountain is in the Himalayan range?

The right order

1 You have finished a week's camping, and it is raining hard, but you have to pack and leave. Write out this list of essential duties in what you consider to be the best order:
   Replace turf on cooking area.
   Fill in pits and latrines.
   Pick up all the rubbish and waste paper.
   Strike and pack the tent.
   Personal packing.
   Dismantle gadgets – plate racks, washing stands, clothes lines, etc.
   Take down store tent and pack stores.
   Pay any bills left over.
2 What vital last job is not on the list?

Letter writing

Write to Outward Bound Trust, 123 Victoria Street, London SW1 to enquire about their courses, qualifications for admission, etc. Write to *The Duke of Edinburgh's Award Scheme*, 32 Bryanston Street, London W1H 7AE for details of this project. Write to Outward Bound Trust to enquire if they lend or hire films about their courses.

For your information and composition

Study these pictures of London Bridge through the ages. Write a composition on the changing face of London Bridge. Head your writing *Over the bridge*

If you live in London you may be able to study a Greater London Council Publication (number 215) showing London Bridge from St. Mary Overy's Church Southwark in 1749.

Research work

You may be able to work in groups to produce a report or a magazine, a series of lectures or a wall newspaper, on the topic YOUTH HOSTELS, or if you prefer work on the *topic holidays* or *adventure holidays* and go outside the YHA facilities. The answers to some of the questions below will provide clues to the sort of research needed to compile interesting and informative material.

How many regions are there for administrative purposes in the English YHA?

Find out something about some of the actual YHA buildings such as St. Briavels in Gloucestershire, Wilderhope in Shropshire, Naughton near Ipswich, the life-boat station in Welsh Gower, and Holland House in London.

What is the total membership at present? (It was already over 200 000 the year the writer went to Skye!)

What is the cost p.a. for membership under 16?

What is the minimum and maximum age for membership?

What is the cost per night to stay at a Scottish Youth Hostel?

Why are there no sheets used?

What rules and regulations are there about arrival and departure at Youth Hostels?

List any other rules or duties.

Who is in charge of each hostel?

Plan a YHA holiday in the Lake District for ten days, working out cost; walking and rail timetable; and full details of places to be visited, mountains to be climbed, etc. (You may substitute a district other than the Lakes if you prefer.) If mountaineering is included, add a brief note on safety precautions.

Refer to some of the following YHA adventure ideas: Rucksack Theatre; gliding; Offa's Dyke and frontier castles; searching for the past; railway holiday; cruising; walking with a purpose, etc.

Sealink research

Trace or copy this map and below your copy add these details (consult a travel agent) for any five of these routes.

The cost for a family of three, two adults and a child (aged 10 years), in a 1100/1300 cc car up to 14 ft (4·2672 m) long.

Project work

1 Copy the chart below. Then decide what you consider to be the user's priorities for each vehicle listed. Use a five-point scale and put 5 in the space for your top priority and 4, 3, 2 down to 1 for your lowest award. Work in groups and compare results.

	Town car	Scooter	Limousine	Sports car
Parking-space				
Mobility				
Economy				
Speed				
Comfort				

2 Copy the chart below. Then decide the priorities for passengers for each vehicle. Use a five-point scale as above. Work in groups and compare results.

	Comfort	Cheapness	Speed	Frequence of service
Local bus				
Long distance coach				
Local train				
Inter-city train				
Airliner				

3 Make a detailed study of your own neighbourhood from the traffic point of view. Write a report under these headings:
Amount of traffic congestion
Provision of car parks and their nearness to shops
How traffic affects old buildings, enjoyment of amenities, etc.
Number of accidents per year (consult police)
Possible solutions (i.e. by-pass)
Your report could be compiled on a group or class basis. Apart from fact-finding, it could be the result of interviews with

(a) people who live or work in most crowded areas.
(b) Parents worried about safety of their children at particular 'black-spots'.
(c) Motorists annoyed/satisfied with parking facilities.
(d) People likely to be affected in some way by a new by-pass, one-way system or revised traffic rules.

Modern living

This mobile shell in which we encase ourselves is lethal as soon as it begins to move. Usually it hurls itself along a street designed for slow-moving horse carriages, and is separated from the pedestrian by a six-inch curb only; both pedestrian and driver are acting mainly on the sub-conscious, for otherwise no power on earth could keep the accidents as low as they are. It can make undesirable noises and when in motion perpetually emits an odour as disagreeable as that of a skunk, able to kill plants at three feet and permanently retard growth for a considerable area around. It requires space at home equal to that of half the living room, and demands aggressively an equal amount wherever it may terminate its journey.

Give the gist of the above passage in a couple of sentences and supply a title.

On the road

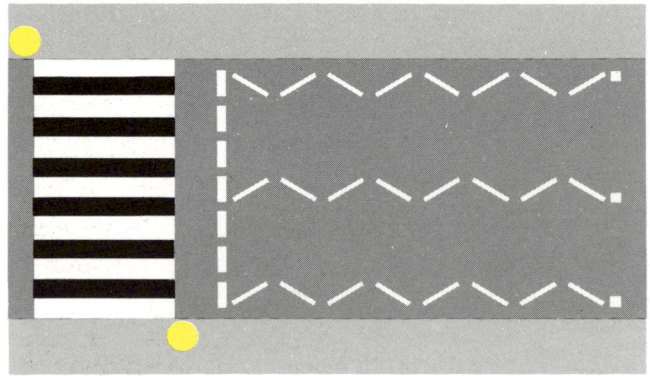

Zebras

What is the purpose of the broken white lines running in zig-zags down the centre and sides of some roads? What laws apply to motorists in this area? What is the purpose of the broken white lines one yard short of each side of the zebra crossing?

Some signs of the times

1 Explain the message in each of the following signs.

2 Refer to an ordnance survey map and check the signs listed below. Then sketch them into your book, using colour where necessary. Now find an example of each on the map you are using. Work in small groups.

Windmill – quarry – wireless or TV mast – glasshouse – viaduct – tunnel – embankment – site of a battle – orchard – youth hostel – church or chapel with tower – PH – MS – TH – PC – wood – bridge.

For your information: London's other underground line

The tiny trains of London's oddest railway look as if they come from Toytown, but, in fact, they are a highly successful example of forward planning.

The trains, 60 of them, belong to the Post Office, which runs its own private underground railway 70 ft below the centre of London. Six-and-a-half miles of track, serving seven stations, are used six days a week to distribute mail between sorting offices and conventional railway stations from which mail is sent to all parts of Britain.

The railway, whose small khaki-coloured one- and two-car trains carry over 45 000 bags of mail a day, is the only one of its kind in the world. Its trains are completely automatic and have no drivers, no guards.

Surprisingly, this railway is no product of our space age, but was planned in 1911 and opened in 1927.

Since then it has needed hardly any alteration. The trains still have their original motors, only one new station has had to be added, and the system of putting the mailbags into containers for easy handling has not been changed at all.

Post Office officials speak proudly of their electric railway. A train carrying mail from the eastern district office at Whitechapel along the six-and-a-half miles to Paddington Station in the west of

Just 70 ft below street level unmanned Post Office trains carry mail unhindered through the heart of London.

London takes 38 minutes, including loading time. A similar journey by Post Office van through London's congested traffic takes 65 minutes – with luck.

The driverless trains work on a very simple principle. The track between stations is electrified and trains, either 27 ft or 56 ft long, can achieve a speed of 35 m.p.h. Immediately before a station there is an electrically dead section of track, which stops the train.

Then a lower voltage (150 instead of 440) is applied and the train moves at 8 m.p.h. into the station. When it gets to the platform power is removed again and the train stops, ready for the postmen on the platform to load and unload the containers.

Stanley Scott, the railway's manager, says that the only improvement he would like to see on the railway is its extension, but the cost of extension is just out of the question.

In 1927 the Post Office railway cost £1 600 000 to build. Today it would cost that to build one new station.

The Post Office can arrange for parties to visit the railway – though no one is allowed to travel on the trains. Parties of children over 12 can be given a conducted tour. Details may be obtained from Mr J Carpenter, 14–18 Old Street, London EC1V 9PH.

The photograph speaks

Tell the story of this girl – mention her feelings, her thoughts, her hopes and her fears.

9. Language study two

Direct and indirect speech and punctuation

1 Explain the difference between these two sentences:
   The doctor said that he would come at once.
   'I will come at once,' said the doctor.
2 Explain the punctuation rules governing these two sentences.
   John complained, 'It always rains in the holidays.'
   John complained that it always rained in the holidays.
3 What changes have to be made to verbs when direct speech is changed to indirect, or reported, speech?
4 Write out each sentence below in direct speech.
   Mr Bumble said that every trade had its drawbacks.
   Mr Weller said that no man knew how much he could spend till he tried.
5 Change this passage from indirect to direct speech.
   The chamber-maid opened the door and told Mr Pickwick that this was his room. Mr Pickwick looked round approvingly and asked whether anyone would be sleeping in the other bed. The maid assured him that it would not be used, whereupon Mr Pickwick thanked her and asked her to tell his servant to bring up some hot water at half-past eight next morning and that he would not want him any more that night. The maid bade Mr Pickwick good-night and retired, leaving him alone.

Change each verb in *italics* into one single verb:
1 Are you sure the bomb won't *go off*?
2 I shall never *give in*.
3 I shall do my best to *make up for* my misdeeds.
4 The volcano *broke out* just as we arrived.
5 Cairns on mountains *point out* the route.
6 Before playing, *breathe in* as deeply as you can.
7 Fleming *came upon* penicillin by accident.
8 He *thought up* a method of blending plastic and aluminium.
9 The angry bull *let out* a roar.
10 You will have to *give up* your claim for a prize.

Write sentences (8 in all) using the following words so as to make clear the differences in meaning.

   misbelieve displace miscolour miscount
   disbelieve misplace discolour discount

The second list below contains words opposite in meaning to the first, but the words are not in matching order. Match the words in the two lists:

   transparent precious modern innocent
   failure attract simplify fertile decay
   alleviate sympathy courage arrival
   occupy hate expand false fierce
   laconic attack

   guilty aggravate cowardice barren defend
   contract opaque success complicate tame
   love departure repel ancient true
   worthless antipathy verbose growth
   vacate

Scrambled paragraphs

In the two pieces below only the first and last lines are correctly placed. The rest are *scrambled*. Write out each piece with all the lines in their correct, *unscrambled* order. The words within the lines are never misplaced, nor is the punctuation incorrect.

Though some historians have doubted this story and
accurate. Pocahontas showed herself a kind,
general opinion now is that it is substantially
untrue romances have been woven around it
generous and able girl and was ever a friend to
Smith and the white men.

Of all the figures in that large family group
Princess Amelia, pathetic for her beauty, her
prettiest, I think, is the father's darling, the
which surrounds George and his queen, the
passionate tenderness with which her
sweetness, her early death, and for the extreme
father loved her.

Word study

Write a definition of each of the following so as to make clear the difference between the members of each group:

river	clock	road
canal	watch	path
lake	sundial	lane
estuary	alarm clock	motorway

Intelligent reading

This section is designed to test comprehension and to show understanding by intelligent *reading aloud*. Take five minutes to study the passage below, and then read it aloud. Elocutionary expertise is *not* required. What is needed is clarity and liveliness, together with a quality of reading which shows understanding for the passage.

Something checked us. Not with a jolt, but with a gentle yielding, and a slight rubbing sound. From where I sat in the stern of the dinghy, keeping a little way on, and steering with a muffled oar, I could see practically nothing in the darkness, but it did not feel as if we had hit the bank.
'What is it?' I whispered.
The little boat rocked as Phyllis clambered forward. There was a faint thud from some part of our gear, dislodged. Presently her whisper came back.
'It's a net. A big one.'
'Can you lift it?'
She shifted. The dinghy rocked again, and then remained tilted for a moment. It relaxed back to an even keel.
'No. Too heavy,' she said.
I hadn't expected that kind of hold-up. A few hours before in daylight I had prospected the route with binoculars, from a church tower. I had observed that to the north-west there was a narrow gap between two hills, and that beyond it the water widened out into a lake stretching further than I could see. It looked as if, once past that neck, one

ought to be able to travel a considerable distance without coming too close to the shore. I traced the way to the gap and memorised it with care before I came down. The tide turned and began to rise before it was quite dark. We waited another half-hour, and then we set off, rowing up on the flood. It had not been too difficult to find the gap, for the silhouette of the two hills showed faintly against the sky. I had moved to the stern to steer and let the tide carry us silently through. And now there was the net . . .

I turned the craft so that the flow held us broadside against the barrier. I shipped the oar cautiously, felt for the net, and found it. It was made of half-inch rope with about a six-inch mesh, I judged. I felt for my knife.

'Hold on,' I whispered. 'I'll cut a hole.'

JOHN WYNDHAM *The Kraken Wakes* (1903–1969)

Reduce these mountains to molehills

A mass of material detached from the earth's crust habitually rotating on its axis will not accumulate an accretion of spongy vegetation.

Individuals who are constrained to inhabit vitreous structures of frangible material should on no account employ petrous formations as projectiles.

A superabundance of technicians' skill in the preparation of gastronomic concoctions will impair the quality of the liquid end-product.

Condensing sentences

Notice how the second sentence in the examples below has been condensed to nearly one-third of its original length, without omitting any fact or loss of effect:

> When he had departed from the house, I began to entertain doubts in my mind as to whether I had been altogether wise in refusing to accept the offer which he had made. (33 words)

> After his departure, I began to doubt my wisdom in refusing his offer. (13 words)

Reduce the following sentences to the number of words suggested after each one:

1   As a consequence of hard study lasting for a period of two years, the candidate was successful in his efforts to pass the examinations which were essential to his career. (12)
2   There are many and varied opinions on the question as to whether work done at home after school is of any great value. (8)
3   Land which is being used for growing crops should be ploughed and harrowed and have different crops planted from year to year. (9)
4   After we had consulted our neighbour who was the sort of person who liked to notice everything that went on, we were able to find out who the person was who had called so mysteriously. (15)

Making a summary

1 Without altering the sense, reduce the following sentences by finding one word to replace those in brackets,

e.g. He felt that his contribution would be (so small that it would hardly be noticed).
He felt that his contribution would be insignificant.

The story was (one people found impossible to believe).

Many of the (people who lived and worked on the farm estate) were provided with cottages.

One of the mysteries of nature is (why birds leave England in the Autumn).

He lived in an area (almost entirely devoted to iron and steel works and manufacturing plants).

(The residential areas on the outskirts of the towns) are spreading farther into the country.

2 Rewrite the passage below in not more than 50 of your own words, using indirect speech. Begin: Mr Micawber said that . . .

'In reference to our domestic preparations, madam,' said Mr Micawber, with some pride, 'I beg to report them. My eldest daughter attends at five every morning in a neighbouring establishment, to acquire the process of milking cows. My younger children are instructed to observe the habits of pigs and poultry, maintained in the poorer parts of this city; my son, Silkins, has issued forth a walking-stick, and driven cattle, when permitted by the hirelings who had them in charge.'

Figures of speech

1 Write out the meaning of each expression in italics below:

Mr Jones sent us on *a wild-goose chase* and, not *to beat about the bush*, we immediately *smelt a rat.* Jack *hit the nail on the head* when he declared that his father always had some *bee in his bonnet* and he was the sort of person who, if he were *asked to play second fiddle*, invariably *got on his high horse* and decided to *paddle his own canoe.* A lot of what Jack himself said must be *taken with a pinch of salt* because he was undoubtedly *a chip off the old block.*

2 In what circumstances might you quote each of the following proverbs?

Hunger is the best sauce.

Don't cross your bridges before you come to them.

It is useless to cry over spilt milk.

You can't get blood from a stone.

A new broom sweeps clean.

Empty vessels make most sound.

You can't eat your cake and have it.

A leopard cannot change its spots.

Don't burn the candle at both ends.

Necessity is the mother of invention.

3 Explain the meaning of the words in italics below:

His reward came *as a bolt from the blue.*

He had *a finger in every pie.*

He was *born with a silver spoon in his mouth.*

We were always hampered by *red tape.*

My father has *green fingers.*

10. On the move – abroad

Old man at the bridge

An old man with steel rimmed spectacles and very dusty clothes sat by the side of the road. There was a pontoon bridge across the river and carts, trucks, and men, women and children were crossing it. The mule-drawn carts staggered up the steep bank from the bridge with soldiers helping push against the spokes of the wheels. The trucks ground up and away heading out of it all and the peasants plodded along in the ankle deep dust. But the old man sat there without moving. He was too tired to go any further.

It was my business to cross the bridge, explore the bridgehead beyond and find out to what point the enemy had advanced. I did this and returned over the bridge. There were not so many carts now and very few people on foot, but the old man was still there.

'Where do you come from?' I asked him.

'From San Carlos,' he said, and smiled.

That was his native town and so it gave him pleasure to mention it and he smiled.

'I was taking care of animals,' he explained.

'Oh,' I said, not quite understanding.

'Yes,' he said, 'I stayed, you see, taking care of the animals. I was the last one to leave the town of San Carlos.'

He did not look like a shepherd nor a herdsman and I looked at his black dusty clothes and his gray dusty face and his steel rimmed spectacles and said, 'What animals were they?'

'Various animals,' he said, and shook his head. 'I had to leave them.'

I was watching the bridge and the African looking country of the Ebro Delta and wondering how long now it would be before we would see the enemy, and listening all the while for the first noises that would signal that ever mysterious event called contact, and the old man still sat there.

'What animals were they?' I asked.

'There were three animals altogether,' he explained. 'There were two goats and a cat and then there were four pairs of pigeons.'

'And you had to leave them?' I asked.

'Yes. Because of the artillery. The captain told me to go because of the artillery.'

'And you have no family?' I asked, watching the far end of the bridge where a few last carts were hurrying down the slope of the bank.

'No,' he said, 'only the animals I stated. The cat, of course, will be all right. A cat can look out for itself, but I cannot think what will become of the others.'

'What politics have you?' I asked.

'I am without politics,' he said. 'I am seventy-six years old. I have come twelve kilometres now and I think now I can go no further.'

'This is not a good place to stop,' I said. 'If you can make it, there are trucks up the road where it forks for Tortosa.'

'I will wait a while,' he said, 'and then I will go. Where do the trucks go?'

'Towards Barcelona,' I told him.

'I know no one in that direction,' he said, 'but thank you very much. Thank you again very much.'

He looked at me very blankly and tiredly, then said, having to share his worry with some one, 'The

87

cat will be all right, I am sure. There is no need to be unquiet about the cat. But the others. Now what do you think about the others?'

'Why they'll probably come through it all right.'

'You think so?'

'Why not?' I said, watching the far bank where now there were no carts.

'But what will they do under the artillery when I was told to leave because of the artillery?'

'Did you leave the dove cage unlocked?' I asked.

'Yes.'

'Then they'll fly.'

'Yes, certainly they'll fly. But the others. It's better not to think about the others,' he said.

'If you are rested I would go,' I urged. 'Get up and try to walk now.'

'Thank you,' he said and got to his feet, swayed from side to side and then sat down backwards in the dust.

'I was taking care of animals,' he said dully, but no longer to me. 'I was taking care of animals.'

There was nothing to do about him. It was Easter Sunday and the Fascists were advancing towards the Ebro. It was a gray overcast day with a low ceiling so their planes were not up. That and the fact that cats know how to look after themselves was all the good luck that old man would ever have.

ERNEST HEMINGWAY (1898–1961)

Speech and drama

In pairs and using gestures and facial expressions read aloud the dialogue between these two men (only the spoken words).

Now read the poem on page 89 and do the same.

The companion

She was sitting on the rough embankment,
her cape too big for her tied on slapdash
over an odd little hat with a bobble on it,
her eyes brimming with tears of hopelessness.
An occasional butterfly floated down
fluttering warm wings on to the rails.
The clinkers underfoot were deep lilac.
We got cut off from our grandmothers
while the Germans were dive-bombing the train.
Katya was her name. She was nine.
I'd no idea what I could do about her,
but doubt quickly dissolved to certainty:
I'd have to take this thing under my wing;
– girls were in some sense of the word human,
a human being couldn't just be left.
The droning in the air and the explosions
receded farther into the distance,
I touched the little girl on her elbow.
'Come on. Do you hear? What are you waiting for?'
The world was big and we were not big,
and it was tough for us to walk across it.
She had galoshes on and felt boots,
I had a pair of second-hand boots.
We forded streams and tramped across the forest;
each of my feet at every step it took

taking a smaller step inside the boot.
The child was feeble, I was certain of it.
'Boo-hoo,' she'd say, 'I'm tired,' she'd say.
She'd tire in no time I was certain of it,
but as things turned out it was me who tired.
I growled I wasn't going any further
and sat down suddenly beside the fence.
'What's the matter with you?' she said.
'Don't be so stupid! Put grass in your boots.
Do you want to eat something? Why don't you
    talk?
Hold this tin, this is crab.
We'll have refreshments. You small boys,
you're always pretending to be brave.'
Then out I went across the prickly stubble
marching beside her in a few minutes.
Masculine pride was muttering in my mind:
I scraped together strength and I held out
for fear of what she'd say. I even whistled.
Grass was sticking out from my tattered boots.
So on and on
we walked without thinking of rest
passing craters, passing fire,
under the rocking sky of '41
tottering crazy on its smoking columns.

YEVTUSHENKO

Discography

La Campanelita (The Little Bell) on BBC Study
record (RESR 32S), side one, tells the story of two
children from South America who travel from their
lonely village through the jungle to the market
town on fiesta day. When lost they are guided to
safety by a wandering spirit (a Duende) who eats
all the things they hoped to sell. But if you listen
to this story and music you'll hear how it all
ended happily.

Creative writing

You are a passenger in a hi-jacked aircraft.
Describe how the air stewardess saves you and the
others in the aeroplane. Poetry or prose as you
prefer. And you could be the heroine (or the hero,
an air-steward) and write in the first person.

Write a script for a 3 minute *Radio Mainstream
report*: Your interview with the heroine.

The poet speaks

The bridge (seen by a Canadian)

Here, with one leap,
The bridge that spans the cutting; on its back
The load
Of the main-road,
And under it the railway-track.

Into the plains they sweep,
Into the solitary plains asleep,
The flowing lines, the parallel lines of steel –
Fringed with their narrow grass,
Into the plains they pass,
The flowing lines, like arms of mute appeal.

A cry
Prolonged across the earth – a call
To the remote horizons and the sky;
The whole east rushes down them with its light,
And the whole west receives them, with its pall
Of stars and night –
The flowing lines, the parallel lines of steel.

And with the fall
Of darkness, see! the red,
Bright anger of the signal, where it flares
Like a huge eye that stares
On some hid danger in the dark ahead.
A twang of wire – unseen
The signal drops; and now, instead
Of a red eye, a green.

Out of the silence grows
An iron thunder – grows, and roars, and sweeps,
Menacing! The plain
Suddenly leaps,
Startled, from its repose –
Alert and listening. Now, from the gloom
Of the soft distance, loom
Three lights and, over them, a brush
Of tawny flame and flying spark –
Three pointed lights that rush,
Monstrous, upon the cringing dark.

And nearer, nearer rolls the sound,
Louder the throb and roar of wheels,
The shout of speed, the shriek of steam:
The sloping bank,
Cut into flashing squares, gives back the clank
And grind of metal, while the ground
Shudders and the bridge reels –
As, with a scream,
The train,
A rage of smoke, a laugh of fire,
A lighted anguish of desire,
A dream
Of gold and iron, of sound and flight,
Tumultuous roars across the night.

The train roars past – and, with a cry.
Drowned in a flying howl of wind,
Half-stifled in the smoke and blind,
The plain,
Shaken, exultant, unconfined,
Rises, flows on, and follows, and sweeps by,
Shrieking, to lose itself in distance and the sky.

J REDWOOD ANDERSON

Reading for meaning

1 How many arches has the bridge?
2 To what does the poet compare the railway
  lines stretching out into the plains?
3 In what direction do the lines run?
4 How does the poet contrast the area through
  which the train is passing with the area waiting
  to receive it?
5 What emphasizes the blackness of the night in
  stanza 5?
6 Do we see or hear the train first?
7 What are the three pointed lights that *rush,
  monstrous, upon the cringing dark*?
8 Pick out words that represent the sound of the
  train.
9 What happens to the whole of the train as it
  thunders under the bridge?
10 Find single words that in their pronunciation
   represent the sound they describe.

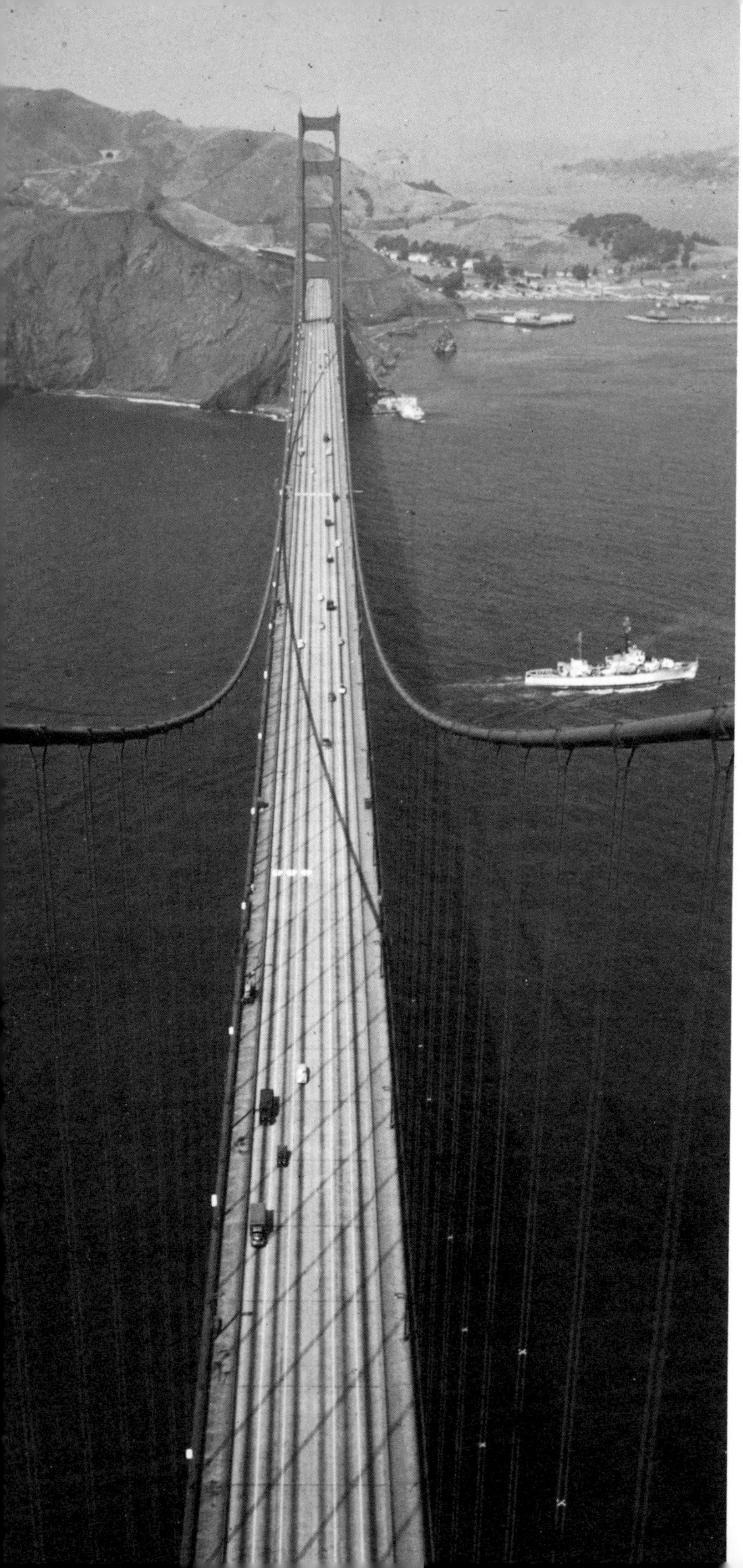

Visual discussions

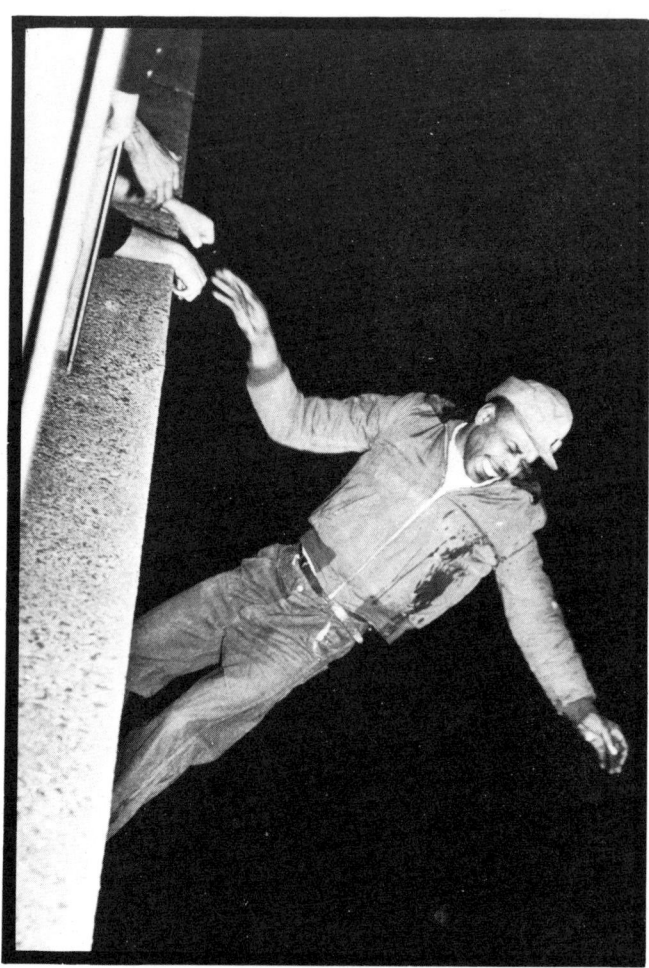

1 *What happened?*
Tell the story of what happened before and after this photograph was taken. Give your story a title.

2 *A view from the bridge*
In this breathtaking view from a tower of the Golden Gate Bridge, traffic crosses the strait connecting San Francisco Bay with the Pacific Ocean.
You are employed as a painter and work on this bridge. Describe your sensations as you look down on this view of it.

Pie in the sky

From the passenger's viewpoint, the captain of a modern aircraft enjoys something of the dignified detachment of the senior physician or the matron of a hospital. On each flight he makes an occasional 'ward round', engaging in brief but friendly conversation with selected passengers, and smiling graciously on everyone else. Then he retires for'ard, and leaves the air hostess and flight steward to get on with the job of keeping passengers comfortable in body and in mind.

At first the purely physical problems seem hardest. Above all, the space problem. For upwards of two months prospective stewards and stewardesses undergo training in mock-up aircraft – learning one by one the vest-pocket techniques which make the most of confined space. You will learn how to put together anything up to sixty meals at a time in a galley where there is not room to swing a kitten. You may be serving between-meal refreshments from a 'bar' which is hardly bigger than the tray on which you carry the duty-free drinks and cigarettes. If someone is unwell, you must cope tactfully, and (if the paper bag was used too late) clean up expeditiously within a narrow space. Passengers can stretch their legs by extending them under the seat in front, but you have no room for manoeuvre.

In an emergency, air hostess and steward are still part of the crew, expected to know all the main routines. They have specific responsibilities – getting passengers into their Mae West life-jackets, for instance. But it is also important to memorise the position of the hatchets and hacksaws which are discreetly placed about the inside of the air-craft, in case it should ever be necessary to cut an exit, instead of using the normal flight doors, the baggage doors or the emergency portholes. You have to remember where to look for the dotted markings which show the places in the fabric of the plane through which emergency holes can be cut without encountering electric wiring or heavy girders.

All this crucial information must lie in the back of your mind, until and unless you are called on to help the rest of the crew to deal calmly and efficiently with the chances of life or death of the passengers in your charge. But meanwhile, the front of your mind must be an ever-ready-reckoner calculating rates of exchange (for orders at the bar) and a gazetteer to say (in at least two languages) how much of the journey is still to come and what that little island is called, just visible on the port bow. You must know how to reassure the querulous – and (though this is more especially a problem for the air-hostess to solve) how to blunt the ardours of the occasional passenger who feels like making a pass. Any spare time may be taken up in holding the baby for a mother who needs a breather.

There are plenty of compensations. Fresh horizons, a glimpse of other people, an opportunity to see the sights. But the price is stiffer than it looks. Once airborne, responsibility never leaves and there is little opportunity to rest and relax. Most working hours are lived in a space about the size of a carriage on the Underground. The view through the windows can seem almost as monotonous; most of the time when you are not seeing a desert of cloudbanks, you see the sea, or the long expanse of green and brown criss-crossed by the snail trails that are the main roads and rivers. In practice, the view is restricted very sharply to the faces of your passengers. Unless you make the most of them – for your own sake as well as theirs – you may find the job a monotony.

If you can keep relaxed and affable after long hours of fuss and bother, and find tycoons an interesting, even an amusing, study, then air-stewarding will probably suit you well.

TONY GIBSON

Comprehension, interpretation and discussion

1 Explain in your own words two ways in which the aircraft captain's job is similar to that of the senior hospital physician.
2 What is the first, and probably most difficult, problem to be overcome by the trainee steward or stewardess?
3 Give a brief summary of their responsibilities in an emergency.
4 List, but do not quote word for word, the everyday duties they might be expected to perform.
5 Explain clearly why *the price is stiffer than it looks*.
6 In what ways is this career rewarding?
7 Is the author trying to encourage or to discourage you from taking it up? Give reasons for your answers.
8 From what you have read above, write a paragraph of your own stating clearly what sort of a person is suited to this career.
9 Suggest ways in which a flight-steward would keep his passengers *comfortable in body and in mind*.
10 Explain an *ever-ready-reckoner calculating rates of exchange*.
11 What is meant by *vest-pocket techniques*?
12 Explain what is meant by the *port bow*.
13 Discuss in small groups the advantages and disadvantages of the work of an air steward or air stewardess.

Looking at words

1 Explain carefully the meaning of the following words as used in the passage (use a dictionary if necessary):
   detachment   mock-up   tactfully   expeditiously   crucial   gazetteer   querulous   ardours
2 By writing a separate sentence for each, show that you understand the special meaning of the italicised word in each of the following expressions:
   selected passengers   *duty-free* drinks
   specific responsibilities   *discreetly* placed
3 Look up the meaning of *tycoon*. What picture of the person does the title suggest to you?
4 From the passage *Pie in the Sky*, find five words which fit the following five definitions:
   hoping or expecting to become something in the future
   a planned and carefully performed movement
   a sudden occurrence demanding immediate action
   a regular course of procedure
   something given as a reward
5 Supply more acceptable phrases for these examples of slack expression:
   to make a pass at someone
   to carry the can
   to be left holding the baby
   to be on to a good thing
   to be in hot water
   to be in a flap

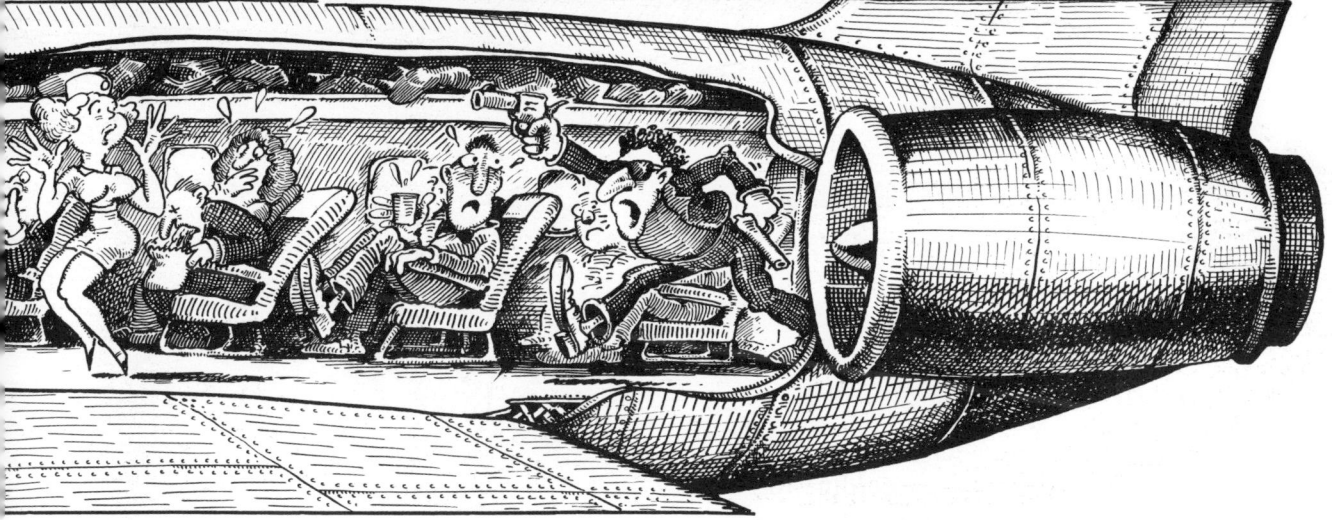

Read, mark, learn and inwardly digest!

When up to 200 people of widely differing designs and desires are trapped inside a metal box and projected through the air at considerable speed for several hours, there has to be some risk of friction. People pick noses, people smell; sleeping people snore and then wake up to pick quarrels with their neighbours; others fidget, get sick and complain about the engine noise or lack of it, the verbosity of the pilot or the lack of data he is announcing, that the cabin is too bright or the cabin is too dark, it's too hot, it's too cold – and where on earth is the large gin and sugar-free tonic they ordered twenty seconds ago. On occasions people even draw guns and hijack the plane.

Hostesses have to rescue false teeth from sick bags, clean up after children, rescue ladies who get sucked into the bowl of the lavatory and cope with any of the nasty situations that can be promoted by that intoxicating combination of fear, booze and boredom. And remember, dear, *smile*.

From *The Sunday Times*

Composition

Answer one of the following:
1 In 10–15 lines, give advice to someone about how to take up a particular sport or pastime or job such as mountaineering, fishing, camping, baby-sitting, paper round etc.
2 Write a short description of a dramatic and horrible journey by air.

Visual discussions

This girl is *not* an airstewardess. Decide what her job is by reference to her equipment. Then tell a story about her.

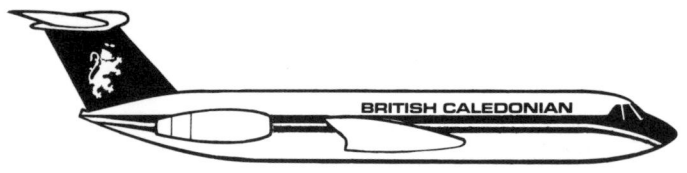

In an emergency

Consider and discuss the following non-verbal,
visual instruction chart to show *emergency
procedures* on an aircraft. Are the diagrams clear?
Say what you are to do or not to do according to
the visual in each of the frames; then write a clear
and concise account describing what to do and
what not to do; head it 'From the alert to safety'.

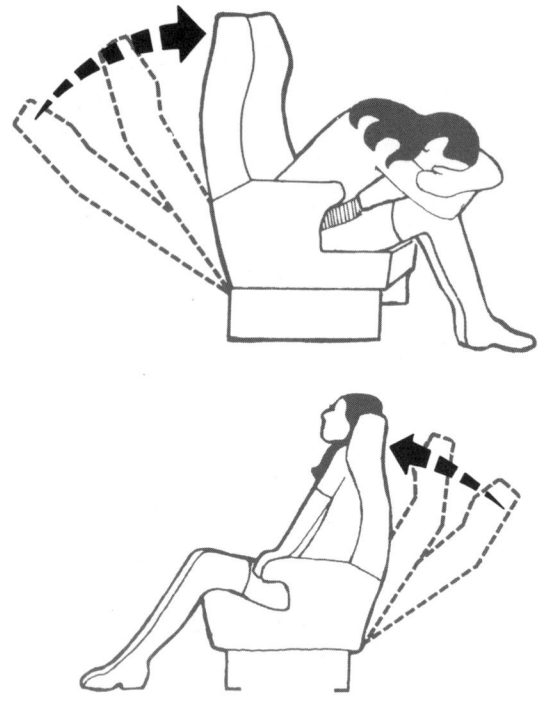

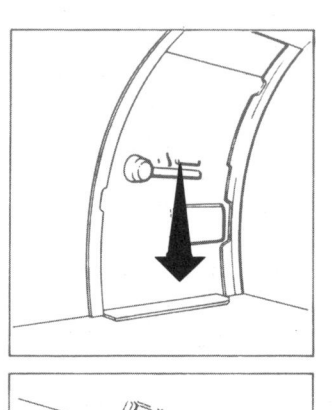
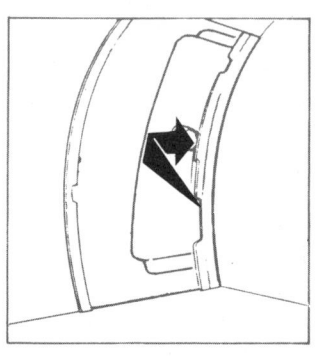
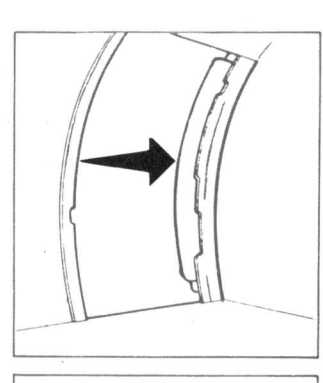
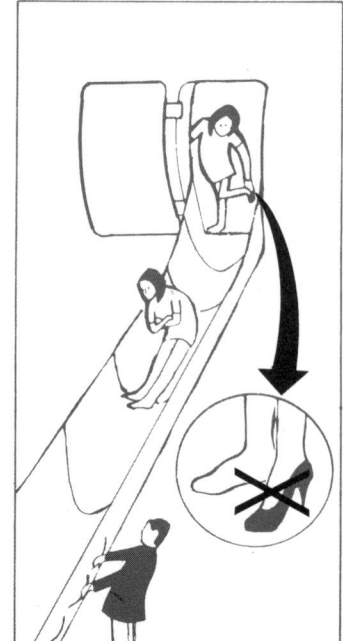
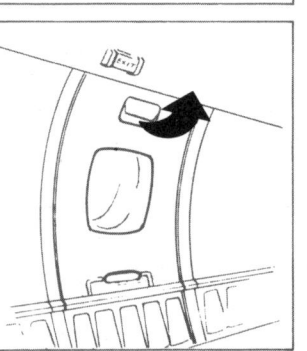

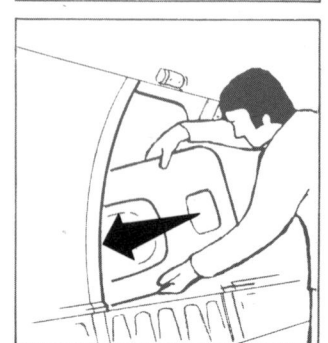

Design centre

Design simple and easily understood visual symbols which could be understood internationally for:

church public lavatory telephone bank post office airport police station hotel discotheque library theatre concert hall camping site

The conquest of Everest and South Pole survey project

Mount Everest (29 000 ft. or 8 840 m. approx) was discovered in 1852 and named after a British Surveyor-General of India, Sir George Everest. Up to 1939 seven expeditions were made to Everest, all of them British. None was successful in reaching the summit.

The three main obstacles they faced were (a) the nature of the terrain (particularly the over-hanging cliffs on the upper part of the North face) (b) the lack of oxygen at high altitudes which so weakened the climbers that they had to rest for several seconds after taking each step (c) the appalling weather (which included 100 mph gales and temperatures 50 °F below freezing).

The first serious attempt to reconnoitre the mountain was made in 1921. The expedition leader was Lt-Col Howard-Bury and one of its members was George Leigh-Mallory, who made the classic answer to the question 'Why do you want to climb it?' 'Because it is there!'

At that time the only approach to the mountain was through Tibet and it was Mallory who accompanied a second expedition on the first serious attempt actually to climb the mountain. He, together with two companions, succeeded in reaching almost 27 000 ft. (8 230 m.) without oxygen.

1924 found Mallory once again on Everest. On this expedition Colonel Norton climbed to 28 125 ft. (8 572 m.) without oxygen. Mallory and a young companion, Andrew Irvine, then decided to make the attempt *with* oxygen. They never returned.

After the Second World War the Nepalese opened their frontiers and made it possible to approach Everest from the south. In 1951 Eric Shipton led a British reconnaissance expedition to find a southern route up the mountain. The route they plotted was to provide the key for the successful assault made later by Colonel Hunt's expedition. Hunt's route (see map) was via the Khumbu Glacier; up the 2 000 ft. (610 m.) high ice cascade, known as the ice-fall; through the succeeding inner basin named the Western Cwm and on across the face of the lesser peak (Lhotse) to the foot of the final Everest slope (the South Col); thence to the summit. Shipton's party, however, got no further than the Western Cwm.

The 1953 Expedition

Lt-Col Hunt was 42 years of age, a Regular Army Officer and a very experienced Himalayan climber. The other members of his expedition were George Band – a student, Tom Bourdillon – a Research Scientist, George Lowe and Wilfrid Noyce – schoolmasters, Edmund Hillary – a beekeeper, Alfred Gregory – Travel Agent, Charles Evans – Surgeon, Griffith Pugh – Physiologist, Michael Ward – doctor, Michael Westmacott – statistician, Charles Wylie – Army Officer, Tom Stobart – camera technician, and Tensing Norgay – Sherpa.

The equipment they took with them included food and cooking utensils, tents, protective clothing, boots and crampons, gloves and sleeping bags, vast quantities of climbing ropes, pitons and pegs, lightweight ladders for crossing crevasses and 160 oxygen bottles. There were no roads into that part of Nepal so every ounce of the equipment had to be carried in by porters.

The main base camp was set up at 18 000 ft. (5 486 m.) on the Khumbu Glacier. From there it was going to take nearly two months to reach the summit and would necessitate setting up eight other camps on the way. But in the later stages of the climb the climbers were expected to need every bit of their energy just for climbing. The transportation of the necessary three tons of food and equipment from base to the further camps would be left to a party of 35 Sherpa porters. Their leader, Tensing, was looked upon as a climber not a porter. Hillary, Lowe and Band reconnoitred the punishing route up the icefall (via Hillary's Horror, Hell-fire Alley and Atom Bomb Area) to camp 4 and it took them nine days. Relays of Sherpas, carrying 40 lbs. each, then took the three tons of equipment to set up camp 4.

It fell to Lowe and Sherpa Ang Nyima to make the first attempt on the Lhotse face. They were climbing without oxygen, which needed to be con-

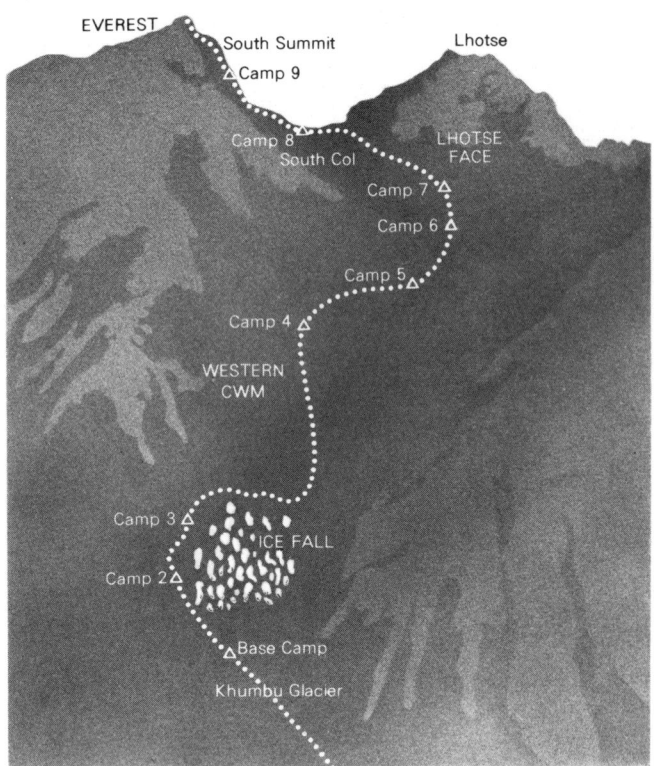

served for the later climbs, and the strain on their lungs was considerable. Colonel Hunt had hoped to spend no more than four days on this part of the climb but after ten days Lowe and Ang Nyima were still 1 000 ft. (305 m.) below the South Col. They were forced to withdraw and Noyce, with Sherpa Annullu (both using oxygen) were sent to complete the climb on the South Col (26 000 ft or 7 925 m.).

Evans and Bourdillon were chosen as the first of the two-man teams to make the assault on the final peak by way of an intermediate peak named the South Summit. They managed to reach 28 700 ft. (8 748 m.) before a defective oxygen cylinder forced them to turn back. On 28th May the second assault team, Hillary and Tensing, set out from the South Col. Lowe, Gregory and Sherpa Ang Nyima went with them, carrying supplies as far as camp 9. Then they returned, *without* oxygen. Tensing and Hillary spent the night of the 28th at camp 9 (27 900 ft. or 8 504 m.) in a temperature of −27 °C. The following day they made their way to the top.

Lt-Col Hunt and Edmund Hillary received knighthoods and Sherpa Tensing Norgay was awarded the George Medal.

Project work: To the South Pole

On the lines of the outline on the Conquest of Everest above prepare a survey entitled *To the South Pole*. Work in groups within the following structure. The map should be copied, and included with the part on Captain Scott's fatal expedition of 1911–1912. Use encyclopaedias and other reference books. Also *Discovery of the Poles* by Riley and Taylor (Penguin).

1 Background information – Make brief notes on: The size of the continent of Antarctica. (Use a globe.) The average summer temperature. Height of the South Pole Region. Bird life and fishes to be seen. Thickness of ice covering the land, etc. The crossing of the Antarctic Circle by Captain James Cook in 1773.
2 Captain Robert Falcon Scott appointed to head British National Antarctic Expedition in 1900. Experience gained, etc. 29 November 1910: ship *Terra Nova* left New Zealand. List names of members of this expedition. What equipment did they have? What food was carried? January 1911: stores disembarked at Cape Evans. Give distance from Cape Evans to the Pole. They crossed the Great Ice Barrier and climbed the slopes of the Beardmore Glacier to the polar plateau – give its height above sea level. Mention methods of transport (the motor sledges proved almost useless).
3 Amundsen's plan and route. Give details of his background (country), where he landed, etc. How many days before Scott did Amundsen start his Polar dash?
   What did the exhausted British party find when they finally reached the Pole on 18 January 1912?
4 The return journey.
   The weather conditions, the state of the supplies, the actions of the men and their leader, Captain Scott. Then drama and tragedy of the party trapped in their tent within 11 miles of One-Ton Supply Depot. 12 March 1912: quote Scott's last entry in his diary.

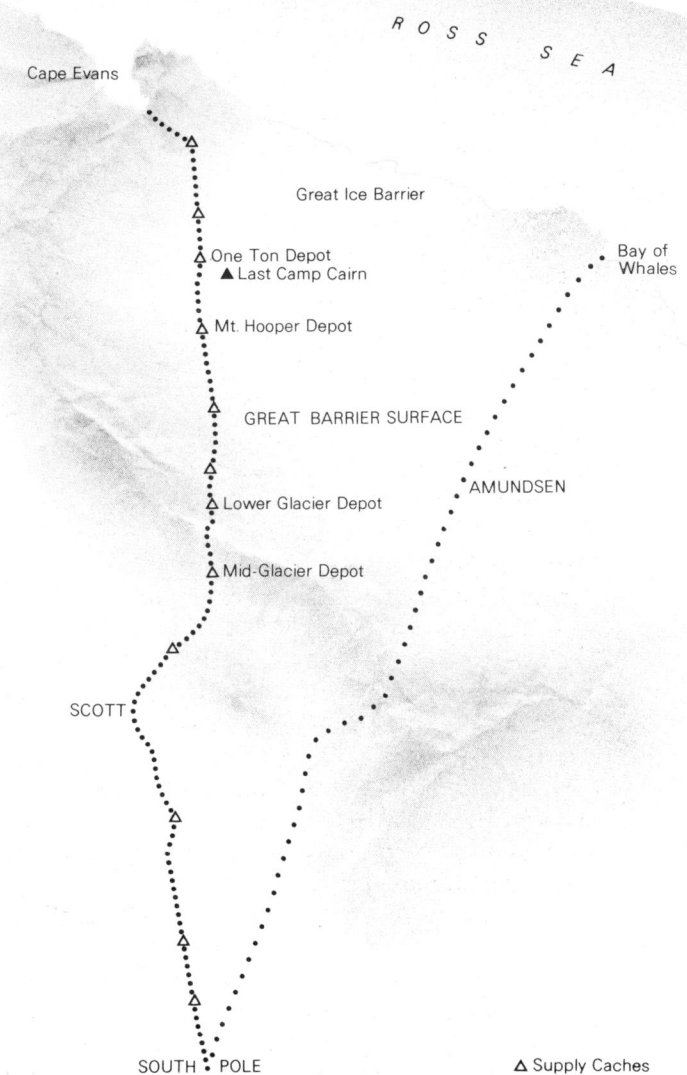

5 More recent events.
   The Commonwealth Transantarctic Expedition. Sir Vivian Fuchs and Sir Edmund Hillary (of Everest fame), etc.

Postscript

Under present-day conditions make a brief report on what kind of foods are most suitable for polar expeditions. What food would provide most nourishment and vitamins for least weight? What types of food are essential for life? Which are luxuries?

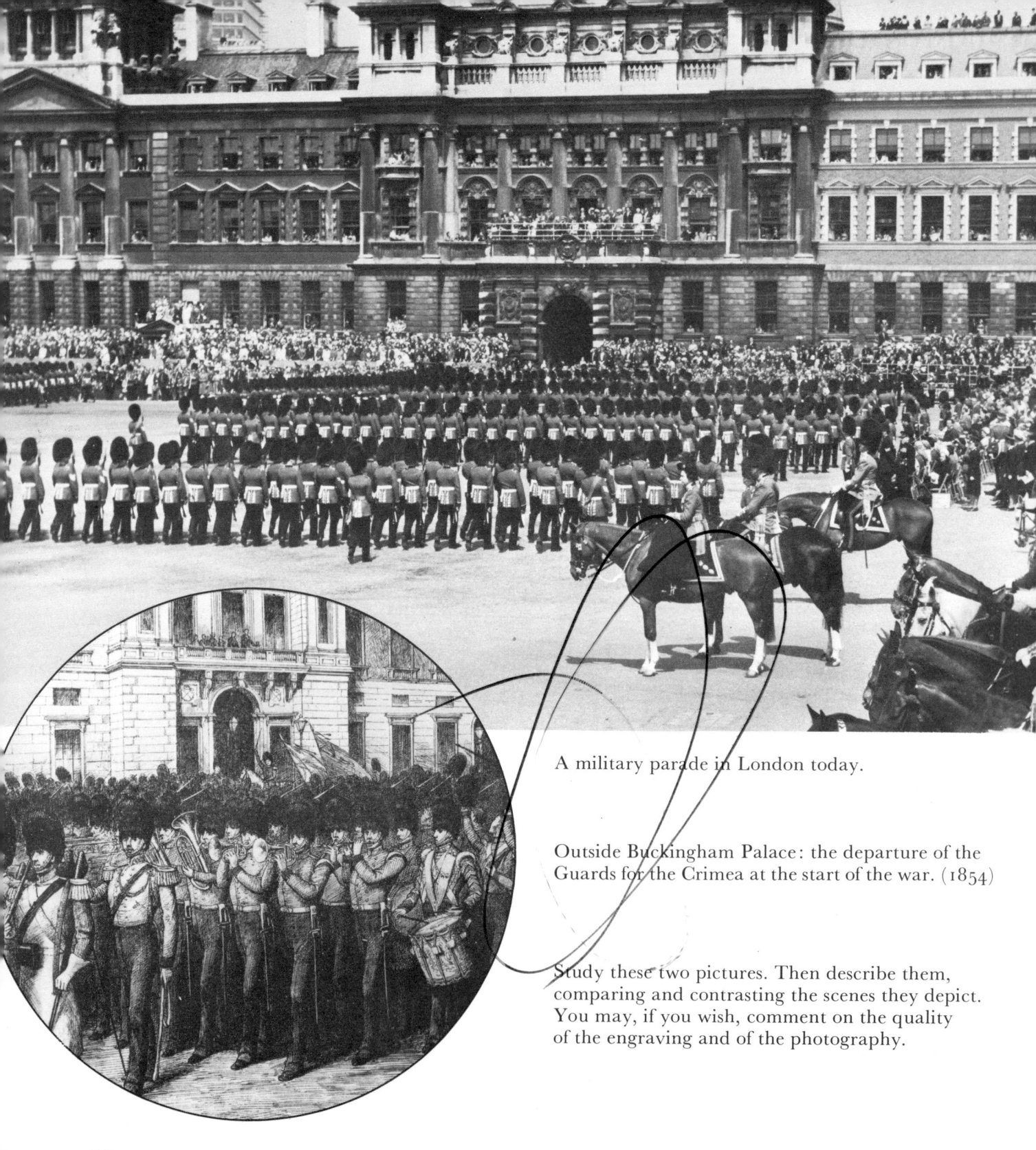

A military parade in London today.

Outside Buckingham Palace: the departure of the Guards for the Crimea at the start of the war. (1854)

Study these two pictures. Then describe them, comparing and contrasting the scenes they depict. You may, if you wish, comment on the quality of the engraving and of the photography.

The Destruction of Sennacherib

The Assyrian came down like the wolf on the fold,
And his cohorts were gleaming in purple and gold;
And the sheen of their spears was like stars on the sea,
When the blue wave rolls nightly on deep Galilee.

Like the leaves of the forest when Summer is green,
That host with their banners at sunset were seen:
Like the leaves of the forest when Autumn hath
     blown,
That host on the morrow lay wither'd and strown.

For the Angel of Death spread his wings on the
     blast,
And breathed in the face of the foe as he pass'd;
And the eyes of the sleepers wax'd deadly and chill
And their hearts but once heaved, and for ever
     grew still!

And there lay the steed with his nostril all wide,
And through it there roll'd not the breath of his
     pride;
And the foam of his gasping lay white on the turf,
And cold as the spray of the rock-beating surf.

And there lay the rider distorted and pale,
With the dew on his brow, and the rust on his mail;
And the tents were all silent, the banners alone,
The lances unlifted, the trumpet unblown.

And the widows of Ashur are loud in their wail,
And the idols are broke in the temple of Baal;
And the might of the Gentile, unsmote by the
     sword,
Hath melted like snow in the glance of the Lord!

                              LORD BYRON (1788–1824)

For discussion

Compare events in this poem with accounts in
the Bible: 2 Kings Chapter 19, verse 35; and
Isaiah Chapter 37, verse 36.

To take you further

1 Now find the poem *The Lady of Shalott* by
  Tennyson and read it.
2 Laurens van der Post wrote a book called *The
  Lost World of the Kalahari*. It is a Penguin. Discuss
  if it is readable or exciting for your age group to
  tackle. Work in groups on the report, or choose
  any other book which deals with real life
  adventure.
3 Appendix two at the back of this book (page 131)
  gives full details of Youth Hostelling Abroad.
  Take a look at it now and make notes for future
  reference.
4 *Film – The Train*
  A 20 minute journey through Sweden: British
  Film Institute, 42/3 Lower March, London,
  SE1 7RG.
5 *Radio Ballad*
  The Ballad of John Axon: MacColl, Parker.
  The BBC documentary recording of the story of
  the engine driver, John Axon (Argo RG 474.
  From Argo Records).

A chance to act – a group activity

Mime or act some of the scenes from the text and
pictures in this unit. Choose suitable background
music and/or make up suitable 'sound effects' from
classroom materials. Select a particular incident
to occupy your classroom stage for about five
minutes. Work from a script if necessary, but
actors may prefer to make up the dialogue as they
go along. A 'narrator' might be useful in some
circumstances.

11. Group C folder work

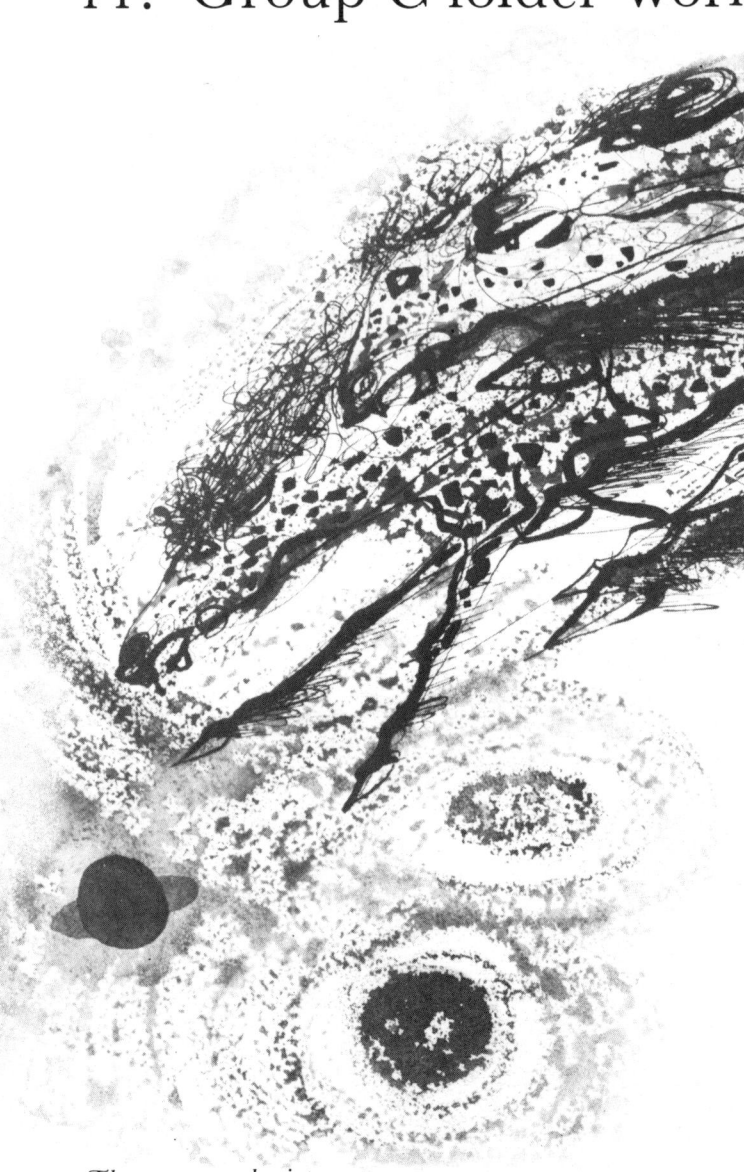

The runaway chariot
by Charles Keeping

Look at the picture by Odilon Redon, *Chariot of the sun*. Study this picture and then read this description:

At first Phaeton was glad and proud to be driving the magnificent chariot of the sun. But soon he began to feel frightened. The horses felt that the chariot was too light to be carrying Apollo; that it was being driven by someone whose hand on the rein was weak. Knowing this, they tossed their fiery heads. They left the track which Apollo had made for them, and set off in a different direction.

Your folio of writing. Attempt some of the following questions (1 to 6)

1 *Visual awareness*
  Compare the picture *Chariot of the sun* by Odilon Redon (1840–1916) with *The runaway chariot*, Charles Keeping's illustration done in 1972. Which one, in your opinion, gives the best *impression* of the story. Justify your answer in writing.

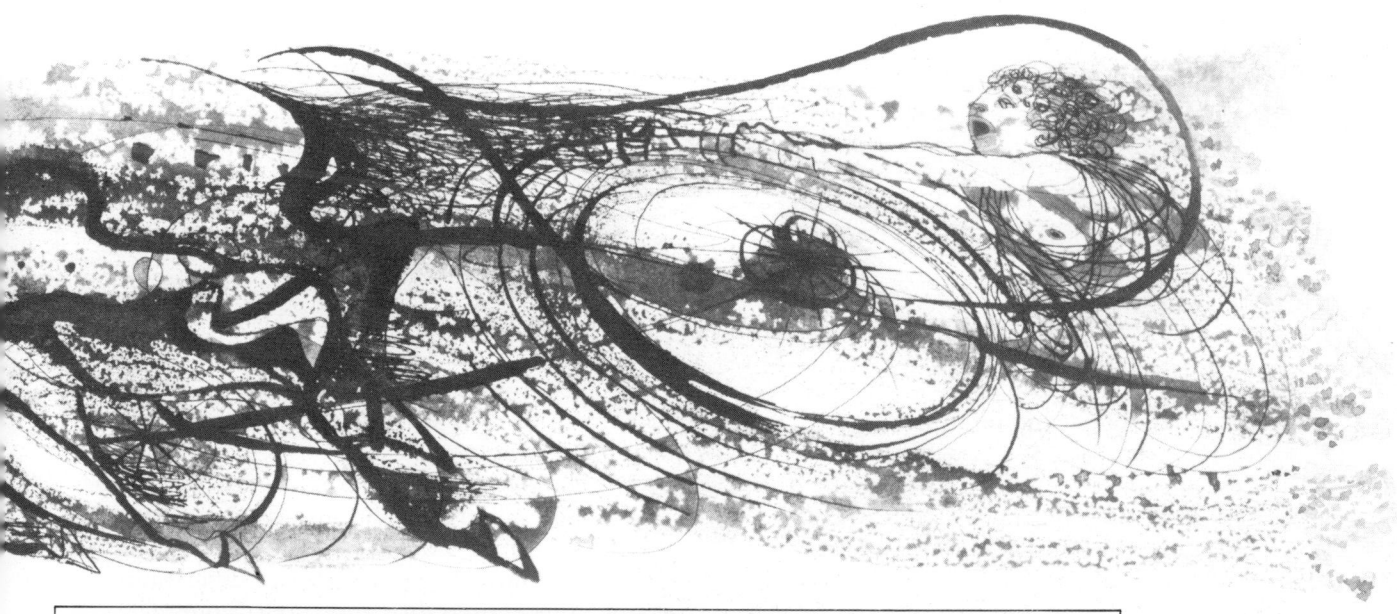

Chariot of the sun
by Odilon Redon

2 Write a few sentences explaining how nearly you think the artist has caught the impression given by the description on page 101. Copy the description first, then begin: 'In the picture, *Chariot of the sun*, the artist, Odilon Redon, has tried to give an impression of Phaeton's awkward situation.' Now go on to describe in what ways the picture fits the text – or fails to do so.

3 *Research work*
Find out and write down the story of Phaeton, son of Helios, and explain why Zeus struck him dead with a thunderbolt.

4 *To take you further – more advanced work*
Notice this definition of *impressionism*:

The theory and practice of the French school of painting used in particular with reference to the works of a group of artists in the 1870s: Manet, Monet, Renoir, Pissarro, Cezanne, Degas, and others. Also applied sometimes to a style of music composition characterized in the works of Debussy, Delius, Ravel, etc.

Find pictures by three of the above impressionist artists. Write down the picture titles and artists' names. Consider the Redon and Keeping illustrations and write down whether you think they are in any sense 'impressionist' pictures in style and execution. (A short report in one paragraph.)

5 *Listening and writing*
Listen to some music by Debussy (1862–1918), particularly *Prelude a l'après-midi d'un faune*

(SXL 6551), then set down your feelings about it in a few sentences.

Listen to one of the present dozen 'top of the pops' discs. Then consider and discuss what impression, if any, the music tries to give you. Or is it perhaps a straightforward description? Name your chosen disc and report your impression briefly.

6 *The artist at work*
Sketch an impressionist picture of Zeus hurling his thunderbolt at Phaeton.

7 *Creative writing*
Give a vivid account of the thoughts that race through Phaeton's mind as his chariot and horses carry him headlong and out of control towards the earth below. Begin, 'Oh, heavens what have I done? Why did I leave my home in Greece?'

Visitor's Britain

Select one of the following:
1 Write a 'Beautiful Britain' advertisement for an overseas tourist. Stress the historical monuments (e.g. Tower of London), quiet villages, homely pubs, lovely scenery. Plan and advertise a tour of part of the country which takes in many of the scenic and historical places of interest. Quaint old customs could be mentioned. A typical beginning could be 'Get in touch with the centuries – visit Britain' OR 'No strangers are

These engravings were made by Thomas Bewick (1752–1828). They show three breeds of dog that you will see today. What breeds are they?

allowed at our Local – we're *all* friends.'
2 Write an advertisement stressing the industrial and scientific achievements of Britain. This would suggest trips to nuclear power stations, steel works, aircraft research establishments, etc.
3 Write a humorous 'tourist guide' for Britain, stressing all the inconveniences, i.e. traffic jams, crowded beaches, long waits for buses, ugly tower blocks of flats, and any other aspect of British life which you do not like.

Further research

There are well over one hundred different breeds of dogs registered with the Kennel Club of Great Britain. The six most popular listed in order are:

1 Alsatian   2 Labrador Retriever
3 Yorkshire Terrier   4 Toy Poodle
5 Cocker Spaniel   6 Rough Collie

Take a 'census' of dogs in your neighbourhood. Compare the order of popularity with the national order above.

To take you further

The Book of the Dog Hamlyn
BBC Blue Peter book of Guide Dogs BBC
Bringing up your Dog by R OLDFIELD Blandford
Guide Dogs for the Blind by D CLEWES Hamish Hamilton

Shorty and the Bank Robbers by J WEBSTER (Rescue Readers) Ginn
All about Obedience Training for Dogs by MOLLIE MALVAY Pelham

Choose a dog

First think over the following considerations before you choose a dog for each of the people listed below.
Will he grow big and need a lot of room?
Will he need a great deal of exercise?
Will he need a lot of care and looking after?
Will he need expensive food?
Will he be gentle with young children?

1 A seventy-year-old widow who lives alone and is lonely.
2 A family with children aged 4 and 18 months.
3 Married couple, no children, who live in a flat in town.

Creative writing: triggers

Write down one of these 'trigger' phrases, then in three minutes write down whatever comes into your mind. Let your imagination flow, and write freely and fast.

Flying through the green ice caverns . . .
I turned the last corner and there . . .
Upside down so the only way to . . .

Skin diving

He ran straight into the water and began swimming. He was a good swimmer. He went out fast over the gleaming sand, over a middle region where rocks lay like discoloured monsters under the surface, and then he was in the real sea – a warm sea where irregular cold currents from the deep water shocked his limbs . . .

. . . He fixed the goggles tight and firm, filled his lungs, and floated, face down, on the water. Now he could see. It was as if he had eyes of a different kind – fish-eyes that showed everything clear and delicate and wavering in the bright water.

Under him, six or seven feet down, was a floor of perfectly clean, shining white sand, rippled firm and hard by the tides. Two greyish shapes steered there, like long, rounded pieces of wood or slate. They were

fish. He saw them nose towards each other, poise motionless, make a dart forward, swerve off, and come around again. It was like a water dance. A few inches above them, the water sparkled as if sequins were dropping through. Fish again – myriads of minute fish, the length of his fingernail, were drifting through the water, and in a moment he could feel the innumerable tiny touches of them against his limbs. It was like swimming in flaked silver.

DORIS LESSING *Through the Tunnel* (born 1919)

Continue this description, using vivid language to describe the skin diver's thoughts and feelings: first as he plunges deeper down and meets huge and friendly fish; then as he realises there is a fault in the oxygen equipment; and finally as he just makes it to the boat above, safe but exhausted.

Library work and research

You are planning to emigrate from Great Britain to Australia, in a sailing sloop provided with an auxiliary engine for use in emergency only. Your boat has provision for a crew of four. Refer to *Selected modern reading* below, then answer the following:

Plan out your intended route and ports of call.

Estimate how long you would expect to take over the journey, giving your calculations.

List the official bodies you would have to notify for clearance.

Draw up a list of essential stores.

List supplementary items which might be useful for barter, and suggest the circumstances in which they might be used.

What spare equipment would you carry in anticipation of loss through wear or hazard?

Selected modern reading

The following may prove enthralling and some may also be useful for the research project above.

JOHN CALDWELL *Desperate Voyage* Corgi

JOSHUA SLOCUM *Sailing Alone Around The World* Collier-Macmillan

THOR HEYERDAHL *The Kon-Tiki Expedition* Penguin

ADRIAN SELIGMAN *The Voyage of the Cap Pilar* Hodder and Stoughton

FRANCIS CHICHESTER *The Lonely Sea and the Sky* Hodder and Stoughton

ANDREW SALKEY *Hurricane* OUP

Monitor: Holidaying in a wheelchair

The Alliance Internationale de Tourisme has compiled information about facilities for the disabled. A team of ten handicapped boys from the Hephaistos school for disabled boys near Reading, Berkshire, with ten able-bodied boys from St Paul's School, London, have taken a look at the situation in Paris, France. They tested amenities for the disabled visitor in hotels, hostels, campsites, sports grounds, lavatories, concert halls, theatres, and cinemas. They also went on river trips, coach tours etc.

Letter writing

1 Write to the *Central Council for the Disabled* 34 Eccleston Square, London SW1 and enquire about their national series of guides to British towns and cities. (Post one letter only.)

2 Write or telephone your local council asking what provision there is for the disabled under the *Chronically sick and disabled act 1970*. Ask if they have carried out a survey to find the number of disabled people in the locality. Ask about free parking badges, and the adaptation of public buildings for easy access. (Post one letter only.)

3 Write to the Automobile Association for their guide for the disabled. (Post one letter only.)

To take you further

Carry out local research in groups and make a report.

12. Crime and detection

Val's perfect crime

'I've just got to have a bike,' said Val to himself during the first week of the Easter holidays. 'If I had a bike I could get out of this dump and away from Shorty's gang and go fishing and exploring, and see the world.'

But the question was, how to get the money? Now Mum was not working, cash was shorter than usual. There had been no pocket money at all lately.

He tried the newsvendors, but they all had boys. Then he went along to see Mr Copley at the stationer's. But everyone knew Val's reputation.

'You're a bad lad,' said old Mr Copley, looking at him over the top of his spectacles. 'Everyone says so. Always fighting!'

'I don't want to fight,' muttered Val, standing sideways to hide a black eye that was fading all too slowly.

'Then why do you do it?' asked the old shopman. 'Look at your coat! It's all ripped. And not a button on it. I want a smart lad.'

Val turned up his arm. The lining stuck out of the cloth. Mum had practically given up mending for him. 'It's a waste of my time,' she had said. 'You ought to go round painted blue like the savages.'

'If the boy you've got now goes, would you take me on then?' asked Val.

'No. I want a steady boy,' said Old Copley and turned away.

Val could not explain that he wanted to be steady, that he hated fighting. No one would have believed him. Then, he was proud, too proud to make excuses for himself. So he rubbed his nose on the back of his hand, and so transferred another smudge of black to his face. Dirt just grew on Val.

Next he tried the grocer's and the laundry.

'Don't you want a Saturday boy?' he asked. 'I'll come evenings, too.'

But they all declared they had boys and the laundry woman cried, 'Go home and wash your face before you go asking for a job.'

Val hadn't thought of that, so he stood there, taken aback.

The woman sniggered. 'Tell your Mum to put you in the next bag wash.'

Being laughed at was too much. Val could feel tears pricking in his eyes, so he ran away with the giggling of the laundry girls still in his ear.

At last he gave up his search for work, and went dawdling out into the yard. 'It's enough to drive you to crime,' he said to himself. ''Tisn't as if I wasn't wanting to earn the money honestly.'

He went off across the Common and down the High Street. He scrumped an apple off a stall, not because he was hungry but as a revenge on a society that did not want him. He went and looked at the lovely, shining new bicycles in the shop windows. They had four gears, pumps, shining bells, carriers – just everything. Val stood there imagining himself coasting down hills, racing along to the sea. And he said to himself, 'It's not fair.'

He began to hate everybody, and to feel the whole world was against him. He hated a community that refused to let him even work for a bicycle. Wandering on, he came to the Supermarket where there was a great crowd of people doing their shopping. They were pressed right up against the stalls, trying to attract the sellers' attention.

I could bring young Len here to do a bit of scrumping, thought Val. I could stand in front of him, and he could pop the stuff in his pocket without anyone noticing. Then he remembered that Len was now eight, and so liable to be summoned as a person responsible for his own actions. Much as Val hated the world, he did not want to involve his little brother with the police.

While all this was going through his head, he was watching a fat lady in a nylon fur coat. She had collected some bananas and a pineapple and was holding them out to be packaged. For a moment she had put down her purse on the counter amongst a bin of apples. Scarcely thinking, but acting on impulse, Val picked up the purse, pocketed it, and dived away out of the crowd. It was done in a second and he was out of sight before the woman had noticed her loss.

So this was what casual scrumping had led to!

Val had thought nothing of pinching a stray apple or a cake, and now here he was stealing money.

Going at a brisk walk, but not really running, he slid into one of the back alleys that ran behind the High Street. The purse was burning in his pocket. He was so scared at what he had done that his mouth was dry and his legs felt weak at the knees. At all costs, he must avoid any tangle with the gang or with the police until he had got safe home and hidden the purse.

As soon as he reached the flat, he locked himself in the lavatory so as to examine the purse in peace. With fingers that trembled, he opened the snap of its inner compartment, and found eight pounds in notes and about eight shillings in silver. Enough money to buy a second-hand bicycle!

He did not feel particularly guilty now that he was safe at home. The lady at the counter had never seen him, and would not be able to describe him. No one else had noticed him, for there was such a crush round the stall. He had really committed the perfect crime.

But while he stood there looking at the money, he realized that there were still complications. He could not go out and buy a bike, for his parents would at once wonder where he had got the money.

What a fool he was! Why hadn't he thought of that before? He left the lavatory, went into his room, and sat down on the bed. He had been a thief all to no purpose. Then suddenly he saw what he must do. He would have to pretend to get a job. This would mean he would have to disappear every Saturday, and on most evenings. No one in the family would have the time or energy to check up as to where he went.

For the time being, he shoved the purse under his mattress. But before he did so, he extracted the odd eight shillings, because it would be nice to buy sweets or cigarettes or even go to the pictures after all these weeks without any pocket-money.

No sooner had Val money in his pocket than he wished to show off, to hint to Shorty's lot that he was rich, a chap who really did things, and who didn't care for the police. But it was rather difficult to think how to convey all this.

As he strolled nonchalantly across the yard, he saw Shorty and Nap smoking by the bicycle sheds.

They dared not attack Val, for Sprot and some women were about. Val got clean away and down the road, but as he came to the tobacconist's kiosk, he had a bright idea. These boys might smoke dull, ordinary fags, but he, Val, would show them! He marched into the tobacconist, and said, 'Dad wants a couple of toofers, please.' Toofers were small black cigars that used to be two for a penny but that now cost about a shilling each. Two shillings was well spent if it impressed the other gang. Dad sometimes did buy a toofer for a treat, so the man in the kiosk handed them over to Val without any question.

When Val got to the Common, he started to get his toofer going. He had smoked cigarettes made up from odd stubs and re-rolled in lavatory papers, but this toofer, once started burning, was much more pungent. Still, anything to impress Shorty and Nap.

Puffing at his toofer like a steam engine, Val strolled across the yard. The cigar smelt so strong that its blue smoke was wafted over to Nap and Shorty. Val did not want to spoil the effect by lingering, but went right across the yard and up the stairs towards his flat. But as he came to the top flight, he suddenly felt so strange and dizzy that he was forced to sit down on a stair, and the half smoked toofer fell from his fingers on to the concrete floor.

Mum found him there as she went out to do her shopping. He was sitting with his head against the wall, his eyes closed and the toofer lay at his feet.

'Cor, Val, whatever . . .?'

He opened his eyes and struggled to rise, but his cheeks were green beneath their layer of dirt.

Then Mum saw the toofer, and asked, 'Where did you get that thing?'

'Someone gave it me.' Even in his last extremity Val could still think.

'Get on!' Mum knew Val well enough to recognize a lie, and with one quick movement she frisked him. There was a jingle of money as she touched his side, and she plunged her hand into his pocket, crying, 'Where did you get that from?'

Val's brain, fuddled by the toofer, moved slower than usual, and there was quite a perceptible pause before he answered, 'I earned it.'

'Come again!' cried Mum. 'That won't wash! You'll come right back to the flat with me, my lord. I've got one or two things to ask you!'

A group of women had collected below them, waiting to come upstairs. When Mum saw nosey Mrs Crawley, she yanked Val up by his coat collar, kicked the toofer out of the way, and marched the boy along to 49. Mrs Crawley and Mrs Doherty exchanged amused glances. Really that Val was a caution!

In the living-room, Mum faced Val. 'Have you been scrumping?'

'No.'

'You have, and don't you lie to me.' She took a step forward, her usually smiling face drawn and worried. 'Where'd you get that money, Val? Give it here. I know Dad and I didn't give you any, so you can't have got it honestly. When I tell your Dad he won't half give you a leathering.'

'Mum! Oh, no!' Val put the armchair between himself and Mum, for in spite of her good temper she could be really angry if roused.

'Tell me the truth!' she cried. 'And give me that money. Where did you get it?'

Very slowly and unwillingly, Val produced the money coin by coin. Three shillings, four. He hoped to keep back at least a couple, but Mum went on waiting with outstretched hand until he had disgorged all of the remaining silver. When she had got it, Mum went on with her catechism.

'Where did you get it?'

'I – I found it.'

'Where?'

Val was feeling too sick to think up a good story, so he came out with the truth. 'In the Supermarket.'

'How do you mean, found?'

'It was on a stall.'

'So, you've been whipping the change?'

'No, no.' All the time, Val had been edging nearer and nearer to the door, so as to be ready to make a dash for it, if he could distract Mum's attention for just one second. But she was too quick for him. She dodged round to the door herself and grabbed his wrist.

'Now, I'll have the truth out of you, Val Berners, if I have to beat it out. Whose is this money?'

Val began to redden. 'Someone dropped their purse.'

'That's another lie,' said Mum. 'Where's the purse then?'

Val saw that he had been silly to mention the purse. 'I threw it away,' he said.

'And that's another lie,' said Mum, who was by now very angry indeed, angry and horrified to find out that her son was a thief. She grabbed hold of Val, crying, 'You give me that purse at once.'

Val fought and struggled to get away from her, but Mum held on tight. 'I won't, I can't,' he sobbed, for he could not let go his only chance of a bike.

'Where did you hide it?' Mum shook him hard, and this on top of the toofer finished Val's defiance. 'If you don't tell me, I'll go to the police and have you put away.'

When at last he confessed it was under his mattress, Mum marched straight to the bed and drew out the purse. The line of her mouth was grim.

'You're a thief, a dirty little sneaking thief!' she cried and slapped him hard across the cheek. 'Your Grandpa and Grandma would die of shame if they knew what you'd done. Dad and me's brought you up honest. We never cheated anyone in our lives, and now look at you! Dirty, low cheat!' Mum suddenly collapsed, the anger died out of her and she sank into a chair and began to sob bitterly.

Val stood by, staring at her, horrified. In all his life he had never seen Mum cry before. She had never before slapped his face. Now she had called him a dirty little sneak thief and a cheat, and all his pride was outraged. He had never thought of himself as a thief. His scrumping had just been an adventure, even his taking of the purse was not stealing, but a revenge on people who would not let him earn money. But Mum had said he was a disgrace, a shame to the family. She had called him a thief. He couldn't be that. He wasn't that. But then, what was he?

'How could you do it, Val?' Mum was sobbing. 'How could you? I brought you up decent. I've done everything I could to give you clothes and proper food. I got up early and went to work, even when I was ill. And now look what you've done! It's all been no good.' And she sobbed more bitterly than ever, feeling the whole defeat, the waste of the bad nights, during Val's teething, her savings spent on his first little trousers, his pop gun, his school shoes, his summer holiday. All she had done for him was sheer loss if he were to grow up a thief.

By this time, the tears were pouring down Val's cheeks, too, making tunnels in the general grime. He turned away from his mother to hide his trembling mouth. He couldn't cry in front of any woman, not even his mother.

'I wanted a bike,' he said. 'All the other boys have got bikes.'

'I'd have given you a bike if I'd had the money,' sobbed Mum. 'You know that, Val, but to steal it – oh!'

'I didn't want to steal for it,' said Val. 'I tried to get a job, but no one would take me. I asked everywhere.' He was walking about the room, banging unseeingly into the chairs and tables. 'They laughed at me – they said – they said . . .' and he was weeping too.

Presently they both got calmer.

'I was so proud of you, Val,' said Mum in a sorrowful voice. 'You don't know. And so was Dad. We both thought the world of you.'

Val had to face the devastating thought that his parents would never be so proud of him again.

ELIZABETH STUCLEY *Magnolia Buildings*

For discussion

1 Why does Val steal the purse? Does he think it is right or fair to do it? Whom does he blame for being unable to buy the bicycle?
2 Does the *amount* of money in the purse make Val's crime worse than if there had just been a few pence? Justify your answer.
3 What does Mum feel about Val? Why is she so upset?

Causing trouble on the football terraces ended like this for these young offenders.

Role playing

Act out some of the following situations – make up your own script. Tape-record and exchange criticisms.

1 Imagine the scene when Val's father gets home. What does Mum say to him? What does Val say? How does Dad react?
2 Imagine you and your friends saw Val steal the purse. What would you do, if anything? Act out this situation.
3 Act out a play based on the title *The adventure that went wrong*. It need not be about stealing at all, but can be based on anything the title suggests.

Film extracts 16 mm.

1 *Bicycle Thieves*
   A poor man's bicycle has been stolen. He and his son see one apparently abandoned – and go to take it – they are stopped and publicly humiliated. British Film Institute: (Study Extract 7 mins) 81 Dean Street, London WIV 6AA.
2 *Billy Budd*
   BFI (9 mins)

3 *Softly, Softly*
   Opening and closing sequences of an episode 'It doesn't grow on trees.' BFI
4 *Young Offenders*
   TV documentary on the problems of being in prison. BFI (32 mins)

Letter writing

Write to your local police station and ask if they will send along their 'home beat officer' to talk to you about crime and detection.

Further reading

STAN BARSTOW *Joby* Michael Joseph
JAMES PATRICK *A Glasgow Gang Observed* Methuen
NEVIL SHUTE *The Chequerboard* Heinemann
J R TOWNSEND *Widdershins Crescent* Hutchinson
D CLEWES *A Boy like Walt* Collins
A FOREST *The Thursday Kidnapping* Faber
M MARLAND (ed) *Z Cars* Longman
M MARLAND (ed) *Softly Softly* Longman
S SHERRY *A Pair of Jesus Boots* Cape
DOUGLAS GRANT *The Thin Blue Line* J Long

'Excuse me, sir, but may I have a word with you about some goods in your bag which you may not have paid for.'

Shoplifting

Examine the picture and read the caption below it. Notice the closed circuit TV camera used for detection.

Consider these statements from *The Daily Telegraph* then answer the questions which follow.

> Loss of goods through shoplifting, staff dishonesty or incompetence costs the grocery trade £27 million a year according to an Institute of Grocery Distribution survey.
>
> Women were thought to make the most effective security staff, they have a discreeter approach, handling suspects less like policemen.
>
> One store manager reported that among those arrested were a former magistrate's wife, a company director's wife and a male security officer. Usually people detected have enough money to pay for the goods.

1 You are the manager of the grocery store shown in the picture. On the closed circuit screen in your office upstairs you saw the events which led up to the store detective's request to have a word with the suspect. Describe the events.

2 The suspect is brought to the manager's office by the store detective. Report the conversation that then took place. End with a stern warning from the manager that next time she will call the police.

3 Mime the events covered in 1 and 2 above. Work in groups and make full use of gestures and facial expressions, especially when in the manager's office.

4 Write an account of *A day in the life of a store detective* (male or female).

Ringing the changes

Before tackling the more difficult exercise which follows, study this dial of an old-fashioned standard automatic telephone. Notice the letters and numbers. Explain briefly how you would dial 999 in the dark.

The following story tells how a notorious swindler and thief was arrested with all his gang just after their most successful coup. It was a pure coincidence that led to their arrest. All the facts are given here, and after studying them you should be able to say what that coincidence was.

The name of the crook was Rapello. His right hand man on this job was a German called Stein, who was on his first visit to England. It was early evening, and they were full of high spirits, celebrating the success of an almost impossible robbery. Rapello gloated over a priceless collection of diamonds, and as calmly as he could, stowed them away from prying eyes. All that remained was to give orders for the well rehearsed get-away to the Continent.

He snapped at the rather more excitable Stein, who was greedily finishing off the champagne, 'Ring Jacko and tell him to have the plane ready in an hour exactly!'

Stein picked up the phone. He was usually the strong-arm of the gang and felt quite compli-mented at being asked to do this. He hadn't used one before in England. 'What number do I ring, Boss?'

'2276.'

'And what exchange?'

'Stanton.'

Superintendent Smith and Inspector Jones of the CID had been working together and were closely interested in the Rapello gang, but had lost all trace or contact with him. On that very evening, the Superintendent had already rung up the Inspector at Barton 6782 to ask if he had any news of Rapello. The Inspector had nothing to report. Ten minutes later, however, the Inspector heard by telephone the exact details of Rapello's movements, and was at the private aerodrome to meet and arrest the entire gang.

There was no treachery, no squealing by any of the gang, no wire tapping of telephones. What was the coincidence that led to the arrest?

Research work

1 Explain, with examples:
  manslaughter – assault and battery – petty theft – in camera – dangerous driving – robbery – mugging – larceny – bigamy – assault – treason – felony – misdemeanour – civil courts – espionage – fraud – embezzlement
2 Would the solution to *Ringing the changes* be impossible if a modern telephone only had been available to Stein? Prove your answer.

For discussion

1 Consider what punishments, if any, should be given for each offence in the list above. Discuss a particular case in which a warning might be more effective than a prison sentence. Then discuss a particular case in which a prison sentence might be more effective than a warning.
2 Is suicide a crime at law? And what is your view?
3 What is the purpose of punishment?

Murder at Denley

Mrs Elvira Vainly of Denley Lodge was found dead at 19.30 by her butler ten minutes after he had returned from hospital where he had spent the day under observation. The police surgeon stated that death was caused by stabbing with a long-bladed instrument. The pathologist established death took place at about 16.00.

Recently, she had negotiated the sale of her estate, valued at £20 000, intending to devote the proceeds to the World Refugee Organisation. By her will, she left the remainder of her fortune, £18 000, to her youngest grand-daughter, Mrs Parton, a poor widow. She left nothing to her two other grand-daughters: Mrs Benstead, the eldest, whom she considered sufficiently well-off as she was married to a successful lawyer, and Mrs Barker, whom she despised for marrying beneath her. The terms of the will were well known to Mrs Parton and Mrs Benstead.

The Chief Inspector investigating the case eliminated the butler. This narrowed the suspects to five members of the family. The following facts from his notebook will help you solve the mystery. You should also use the map.

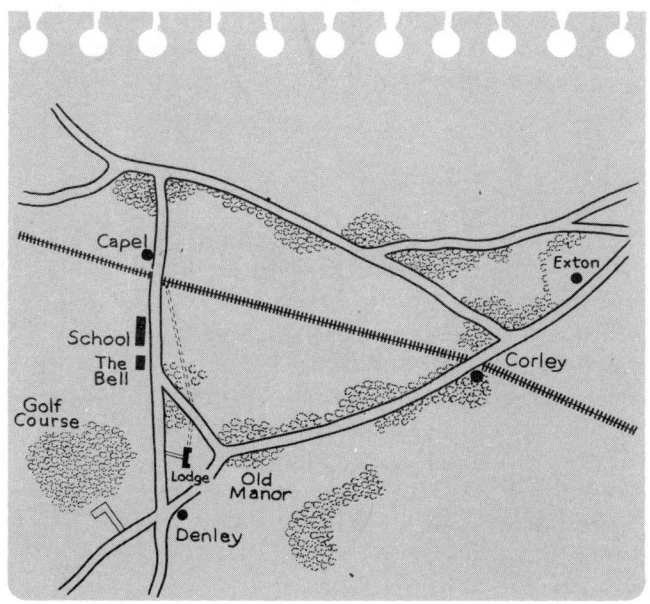

Suspects

Mr and Mrs Benstead live well in a large house at Capel, seven miles by road from Denley Lodge. Mr Benstead is a successful lawyer.

Mr and Mrs Barker live rather less well at Capel, on good terms with the Bensteads. Mr Barker is estate manager at the Lodge.

Mrs Parton lives in a cottage in Denley, about two miles from the Lodge.

Movements on the day of the murder

Mr Benstead left home by car at 10.00 to drive to court at Exton, 15 miles by road from Capel. His case was heard at 11.00 and successfully completed at 12.30. He lunched with his client, and left in good spirits for Denley Golf Club at 14.25. After picking up the landlord of the 'Bell' on the Capel-Denley road at 14.50, he started playing golf at 15.30. Later, at 18.45, he was collected by Mrs Benstead in his own car and driven home, in good time to catch the 19.30 train to London so that he could fly to Cairo that night.

Mrs Benstead caught the 12 noon train to Corley, visited her dentist at 12.30, caught the 13.15 bus to Denley, went to the Golf Club for drinks, picked up her husband's car and drove home by way of Denley Lodge in order to deliver a parcel for the deceased who was then alive. Arrived home at 15.40. Met Mr Barker coming down the drive and invited him in. He left at 16.00.

Mrs Parton caught the 15.00 bus to Corley. Was recognised boarding it. Went to market. Next seen coming out of Capel station at 16.40 by her sister, Mrs Benstead, who was at the station arranging for her husband's luggage to be delivered for his trip abroad. Went back to tea with Mrs Benstead and accepted a lift to Denley where Mrs Benstead returned to fetch her husband from the Golf Club.

Mrs Barker travelled with Mrs Benstead to Corley that morning. Was at the hairdresser's until 14.35. Stated that she caught the next train to Capel station. Walked along the Denley road as far as the school to meet her twin children at 16.00. Failed to meet them and returned home. Was seen at the bus stop at 16.40. Discovered that the children had gone to tea with friends.

114

Time tables
Buses (hourly service)

Denley	8.00	Exton	9.00
Old Manor	8.12	Corley	9.15
Corley	8.35	Old Manor	9.38
Exton	8.50	Denley	9.50

Denley–Capel (every 20 minutes – duration 20 minutes)

Trains

Capel	07.00	08.30	10.00	12.00	15.30	17.00
Corley	07.25	08.55	10.25	12.25	15.55	17.25
Corley	09.00	10.30	12.00	13.30	16.15	17.45
Capel	09.25	10.55	12.25	13.55	16.40	18.10

1 Working in groups eliminate two suspects and find which one was not telling the truth. Justify your answers.
2 Then write an explanation of which suspect you would charge with murder and why. Give a careful account of your reasoning and deal with facts only.
3 Write a story called 'Murder at Denley' based upon these facts but including the arrest and confession of the guilty party. Remember you must prove (a) a motive (b) that the person could have done it.

Discography

Pretty Boy Floyd (Dust Bowl Ballads) Woody Guthrie RCA Victor RD 7642
Chorus from the Gallows Ewan MacColl Topic 12T16
We shall overcome Pete Seeger CBS BPG 62209
Dear Kindly Sergeant Krupke (from West Side Story)
Oxford Town from *Freewheelin'* Bob Dylan CBS BPG 62193

Book list

RAY BRADBURY *The Day it Rained Forever* Corgi
JOHN WYNDHAM *The Day of the Triffids* Penguin
NEVIL SHUTE *On the Beach* Penguin

Read this passage from *Saved* by Edward Bond:

FRED	No luck?
MIKE	Wouldn't feed a cat.
LEN	Waste a time.
MIKE	Same 'ere.
FRED	Got a breeze up.
MIKE	What yer doin'?
FRED	Now?
MIKE	Yeh, t'night.
FRED	Reckon anythin'?
MIKE	Bit a fun.
FRED	Suits me.
MIKE	You're on.
FRED	Up the other end?
MIKE	'Ow's the cash?
FRED	Broke. You?
MIKE	I'll touch up the ol' lady.
FRED	Get a couple for me.

For discussion

Explain, with examples:
1 'Language is pared down to a phrase or two or a word or two. It is an understood code.'
2 'What a distance we have come from the flat well-mannered banter, the dehumanized upper-class voices of the stage plays of a few years ago.'

A chance to act – work in pairs

1 Fred holds a fishing rod out in front of him. He wears jeans and an old dull leather jacket. Len sits beside him on a small tin box. On the ground there are a bait box, odds and ends box, milk bottle, sugar bottle, flask and net.
Now make up your own movements and noises as you speak the lines from *Saved* above.
2 Make up the dialogue as it might be spoken by Len and Fred if they were upper-class students at a fee-paying, private school nearby.
3 Act out and speak the 'upper-class' dialogue.

Language study: situational English

1 Consider this written statement by a burglar:
> My intentions to invade the larder were frustrated owing to the apartment being occupied by several members of the canine persuasion. Being anxious to retain my nether extremities in a state of preservation, I vacated the apartment in question.

Now 'translate' it in a form of question and answer between the burglar and his mate in the style of the passage by Edward Bond from *Saved* above.

2 Translate this 'rhyming slang':
> If one came in through the Rory O'Moore and sat down to dine with one's trouble and strife at the Cain and Abel, one would be in a proper two and eight if one found that there was no Uncle Fred, wouldn't one?

3 Criticise and correct the following:
> Persons normally resident in buildings wholly or partly constructed of glass should bear constantly in mind the potential repercussions of stone projection.

4 Rewrite the following in straightforward and everyday English:
> I regret that the Survey Officer who is responsible for the preliminary investigation as to the technical possibility of installing a telephone at the address quoted by applicant has reported that owing to the shortage of a spare pair of wires to the underground cable (a pair of wires leading from the point near your house right back to the local exchange and thus a pair of wires essential for the provision of telephone service for you) it is a technical impossibility to install a telephone.

5 Use each of the following expressions in sentences of your own:

on the point of	not my strong point
point of view	come to the point
by fits and starts	up to the eyes
head over heels	turn over a new leaf
take a breather	grasp the nettle.

Creative writing

1 Consider the situation in the picture above. Now make up the dialogue which follows this moment. **You can leave your story (which the dialogue will develop) in mid-air and let someone else take it on from where you left off.**

2 Make up the whole story of which the above is just one incident.

3 Make up a story based on the picture below.

Reading for pleasure and reading aloud

The new pack of cards lay in the centre of the green baize.

James Bond leant forward in his chair and studied his opponent through narrowed eyes. As he stripped the film wrapping cover from the cards and threw it aside the hard eyes in the grey face opposite him stared disapprovingly through thick, steel-rimmed spectacles.

Bond placed the cards carefully back on the table, and cut them.

A black seven.

The podgy, ringless hand of his opponent reached out and did the same.

The knave of spades.

Bond picked up the glass which stood at his elbow, and drank deeply. The white, milky fluid ran through his veins like liquid fire. Shrugging off the disadvantage of losing the deal, he picked up his cards without a glance and arranged them in his hand. The smooth coolness of the pasteboard felt good between his fingers as he led his first card.

The nine of hearts. Not good, but there was nothing else he could do.

His opponent countered with the three of spades. Bond played again.

The tension in the room rose until it was almost a tangible thing. Bond could see tiny drops of sweat forming on his opponent's upper lip. He smiled grimly to himself. His adversary might have the advantage of 50 years' experience, but to Bond, the game was a matter of life or death.

He played again. The five of clubs. He glimpsed the dark markings of his opponent's card just before it reached the table, and his heart-beat quickened.

The four!

He noticed that his own hand was trembling slightly, and pushed away his glass in order to gain time.

His next card was the ten of diamonds. The pace was getting hot.

At this stage, Bond couldn't afford to take any risk. He dropped his eyes to his opponent's hands.

The strong, efficient fingers moved like a snake striking, and a blaze of colour lay on the green baize.

A court card! A red king!

Bond swallowed. Everything depended on his next card. All his muscles moved in unison as he flicked it over on to the table.

The king of clubs!

He saw his opponent's mouth opening to speak. 'Snap!' shouted James Bond.

Grannie laid her cards down philosophically.

'You take it all too seriously, James,' she sighed. 'Now finish up your milk and go to bed.'

She shook her head dubiously. She sometimes wondered whatever would become of him when he grew up.

To take you further

1 Look up the meaning of *parody* in a dictionary.
  Then explain in what sense the above is a parody.
2 Find out a few facts about James Bond. In what sense was he 'larger than life'?

Reading for meaning and making a summary

Read this short passage from The Flying Stars, one of G K Chesterton's *Father Brown Stories,* then answer the questions below it:

Well, my last crime was a Christmas crime, a cheery, cosy, English middle-class crime; a crime of Charles Dickens. I did it in a good middle-class house near Putney, a house with a crescent of a carriage drive, a house with a stable by the side of it, a house with the name on the two outer gates, a house with a monkey tree.

1 What is the connection between the reference to Charles Dickens and a Christmas 'crime'?
2 Explain *a crescent, a monkey tree.*
3 What evidence is there which leads one to believe the house-owners had no car?
4 Suggest a title for this passage.
5 Discuss *English middle-class* in the context of this passage.
6 Summarise G K Chesterton's paragraph in not more than 30 words. (Use your own words.)

Composition work

Write a story beginning: *Well, my last crime was . . .*

The poet speaks

These two poems, the first by William Blake (1757–1827), the second by Thomas Hardy (1840–1928), may be said to have a message. What is the message? Do you agree with it?

1 Poison tree

I was angry with my friend,
I told my wrath, my wrath did end;
I was angry with my foe,
I told it not, my wrath did grow.

And I water'd it in fears,
Night and morning with my tears;
And I sunned it with smiles,
And with soft deceitful wiles.

And it grew both day and night,
Till it bore an apple bright;
And my foe beheld it shine,
And he knew that it was mine.

And into my garden stole
When the night had veil'd the pole:
In the morning glad I see
My foe outstretch'd beneath the tree.

2 At the railway station, Upway

'There is not much that I can do,
For I've no money that's quite my own!'
Spoke up the pitying child –
A little boy with a violin
At the station before the train came in, –
'But I can play my fiddle to you,
And a nice one 'tis, and good in tone!'

The man in the handcuffs smiled;
The constable looked, and he smiled, too,
As the fiddle began to twang;
And the man in the handcuffs suddenly sang
With grimful glee:
'This life so free
Is the thing for me!'
And the constable smiled, and said no word,
As if unconscious of what he heard;
And so they went on till the train came in –
The convict, and boy with the violin.

Describe this scene in detail, e.g. food, drink, clothes, furniture, sports equipment etc. Can you see the parson and the shepherd lad in his gaiters?

Other media

1 *Films* (16 mm)
The Rebels, On the Waterfront, 30 mins, BBC TV
Enterprises, Villiers House, Haven Green,
London w5 2PA.
The Third Man, 12 mins, BFI. British Film
Institute, 42/43 Lower Marsh Street, London SE1 7RG.
Violent Playground, 10 mins, BFI.
Twelve Angry Men, 20 mins, BFI.
Paths of Glory, 10 mins, BFI.
The Defiant Ones, 11 mins, BFI.
The Rocking Horse, 25 mins, BFI
Billy Budd, 9 mins, BFI.
Lord of the Flies, 10 mins, BFI.
Young offenders, 32 mins, BFI.
Compulsive Car Thief, 28 mins. Concord
Films Council, Nacton, Ipswich, Suffolk.
Prison Reform, 30 mins, CFC.
Women in Prison, 35 mins. CFC.
The left-handed Gun, 111 mins, Warner. Warner
Pathé Distributors Ltd., Warner Pathé House,
135 Wardour Street, London w1V 4AP.
Loneliness of the Long Distance Runner, 104 mins,
Rank. Rank Film Library, P.O. Box 70, Great
West Road, Brentford, Middx.

2 *Paintings and Photographs*
Van Gogh, Courtyard of a prison, *Vincent van Gogh*,
Phaidon Press p. 97.
Honore Daumier, Deux Voleurs. *A Treasury of
Great Prints*, Peter Owen or *Voices II* (Penguin)
p. 145.
Policeman arresting a demonstrator, David Clarke.
Insight through English, plate 15. Oliver & Boyd.

3 *Discography*
Ewan MacColl & Peggy Seeger, *Chorus from the
Gallows*, Topic 12T16. Topic Records Ltd.,
27 Nassington Road, London w1P 7LD.
Dominic Behan, *Peelers and Prisoners*, Topic 85.
Sound Effects from London tape studios: All Souls
School, Foley Street, London w1P 7LD.
27/28 Demolition. Glass crashes.
55/56 Machine guns. Telephone.
65/66 Cell door. Police Car. Police launch.
Car door, etc.
67/68 American police cars. Car Crash. Footsteps,
etc.

Creative writing

Visit a bookshop or your school or public library
and examine some of the books which have
attractive jackets (dust covers). Then look at the
inside front flap and the inside back flap. You will
notice there a brief statement about the contents
of the book and this is designed to spur the reader
to buy or borrow and read it. There is often a note
about the author as well. The whole jacket is
usually illustrated. With these ideas in mind:
1 Invent a book title, fiction or non fiction, and
   write about 15–20 lines for the inside flap of
   your book, to tempt someone to buy or to
   borrow it.
2 Describe in about 7–10 lines how the jacket of
   this book might be illustrated.
3 Give a brief note on the author (yourself?) in
   about 10 lines for the inside back flap.

13. Group D folder work

How honest are you?

First copy the questions then put the letters with your answers in the boxes on your own sheet of paper.

You are travelling on a bus. Would you:
(a) make no effort to pay if the conductor missed you accidentally?
(b) seek him out and pay your fare?
(c) deliberately try to get away without paying?

You are going to a cinema. Would you:
(a) get in without paying if you could?
(b) pay for a cheap seat and try to get into a more expensive one?
(c) take the seat you had paid for?

Whilst out shopping you see someone shop-lifting. Would you:
(a) ignore it because you didn't want to get involved?
(b) stop the thief?
(c) report what you had seen to the manager?

You call at the lost property office to see if they have the umbrella you left on the bus. They have not got yours. Would you:
(a) select a better umbrella and say it was yours?
(b) admit that yours was not there?
(c) complain that they had an inefficient lost property office?

You give a shopkeeper a 10p piece for goods costing 4p and he gives you 46p change. Would you:
(a) tell him he had given you too much change?
(b) keep the change?
(c) tell him you had given him a £1 note?

You find an extra packet of tea which you have not paid for in your grocery order. Would you:
(a) convince yourself that it was a present from the grocer?
(b) use it and pay for it next time you went in the shop?
(c) ask the shopkeeper to call and collect it?

The boss has mistakenly praised you for a good piece of work which has in fact been done by someone else. Would you:
(a) accept the praise and ask for a rise?
(b) say nothing?
(c) point out that someone else had done the work?

(For answers and scoring, turn to page 124.)

Composition

Describe in about 10–14 lines one of the following:
1 A useful object of equipment for a kitchen or for a craft workshop.
2 Some object as seen under a microscope.

Police report

Write a report for a few days by a policeman 'on the beat' at night. Head your report *A week on the beat by P C Wren*.

First enter details in his own notebook – names, addresses, descriptions, etc., then write a fuller report from these notes.

Here is a list of possible events or matters that may concern him:

Theft of cars (he is given the numbers of cars stolen in his area before going on duty)

Pickpockets, particularly in crowds

Burglary (robbing houses between 9 p.m. and 6 a.m.)

House-breaking (robbing houses between 6 a.m. and 9 p.m.)

Fights, disorderly conduct and drunkenness

Obstruction – of pathways etc.

Lost children

Stray dogs

Car and other accidents – may involve giving first aid

Drowning

Suspicious behaviour

Smash and grab raids

Traffic control in an emergency

Unlicensed cars

Poaching

Tramps or gypsies

Quarrels or fights in private houses

Animal diseases

Paragraphing and summary

The following are notes on the main points taken from a report on *Juvenile delinquency and the law* by A E Jones.

Misbehaviour amongst village and middle-class town children is less common than amongst those from poorer crowded city districts.
Public opinion is responsible for this.
Children do not like being different.
If they are brought before the magistrates they suffer general disapproval.
In slum areas, they have a bigger chance of meeting delinquents.
They are subjected to bad influences.

Now rewrite the information given above, in your own words as far as possible, as *one* well-connected paragraph of not more than 80 words, and not less than 70 words.

The photograph speaks

Turn back to the photograph on page 82 and study it carefully. Now make notes for a photographic competition designed to show one of the following: (The photograph alone must give the message.)
joy   fear   tenderness   humour   fatigue
success   failure   arrogance
Then set your scene and take your photograph.

For your information and report

A few years ago the police listed these causes for the 65 210 accidents in which car drivers were involved. Look through the list, then answer the question that follows.

Fault	Accidents
Crossing without due care at a road junction	11 174
Turning right without due care	8 691
Excessive speed having regard to conditions	5 307
Misjudging clearance, distance or speed	4 773
Overtaking improperly on off side	4 385
Inattentive or attention diverted	3 675
Driver negligently opening side door	2 682
Stopping suddenly	2 549
Failing to comply with traffic sign or signal	2 419
Failing to keep to near side of proper traffic lane	2 403
Losing control	2 358
Swerving	1 740
Following another vehicle too closely	1 606
Turning left without due care	1 548
Failing to stop at pedestrian crossings	1 223
Learner driver	1 185
Pulling out from near side without due care	902
Dazzled by lights of another vehicle	891
Reversing negligently	877
Other error of judgement or negligence	863
Under the influence of drink or drug	642
Negligently turning round in road	519
Cutting in	499
Inexperience in use of vehicle at time	372
Fatigue or sleep	273
Moving off without taking proper precautions	263
Illness	230
Changing traffic lane without due care	180
Hampered by passenger, animal or luggage	49

Compile a report on the accidents in your locality over a set period of time, say six months. Find out from police or newspaper reports the alleged causes of some of these accidents.

Crime and punishment: your own views and research work

Answer any **two** questions:

1 Is a person who has it in mind to commit murder for gain or for hate more likely to be deterred by the death penalty or by a life sentence? Write your answer in not more than 100 words and include reasons for your views.
2 What were the consequences of the abolition of the death penalty in Britain? What has happened in other countries where it has been abolished? Write your answer in note form with headings.
3 Should the police be armed? Justify your answer in one paragraph.
4 Did the existence of the death penalty in Northern Ireland deter murders and check armed violence during the 'troubles' there between 1969 and 1973, when the death penalty was abolished? What happened after 1973? Aim to give figures and try to explain your findings briefly.
5 Use diagrams and notes to show how the breathalyser is used in Britain. Has it helped to stop drunken driving? – give figures if possible.
6 List what you consider to be the 4 most serious driving offences shown on the page opposite. (Place the most serious first.) Now devise a suitable punishment for each of the offences in your list.

The last word

aw nuts aw go peddle yer papers
where did ja cop dat monkeyface
   jeez ja see dat skirt
   did ja glom dat moll
who was tellin you we wuz brudders
how come ya get on dis side deh street
go home and tell yer mudder she wants yuh
chase yer shadder aroun deh corner
yuh come to me wid a lot uh arkymalarky
   a bing in de bean fer you yeah
how come ya get on dis side deh street
go home and get yer umbreller washed
   den get yer face lifted
dis corner is mine – see – dis corner is mine
gwan ja tink ya gonna get dis f'm me fer nuttin
   nobody gets nuttin fer nuttin
   gwan monkeyface peddle yer papers
ya can't kiss yerself in here dis is all fixed

                   CARL SANDBURG (1878–1967)

Discuss any problems of translation and meaning.

14. Language study three

Letter writing

Write two of the following letters. Make up a sensible address for the envelope, and put your school address at the top of your letter.

To a farmer asking for permission to camp on his land.
To your local newspaper asking for help in tracing a lost pet.
To the *Trades Alphabet* asking for more information and booklets about Tea for a project.

Language study

1 Explain why the conclusion to these two sets of statements does not necessarily follow:
   A professional plays for money.
   Bridge players play for money.
   Therefore bridge players are professional.

   All birds have two feet.
   This creature has two feet.
   This creature must be a bird.

2 Supply a correct conclusion to these lines of thought:
   All rats are vermin.
   Vermin should be destroyed.

   Fish cannot live out of water.
   This creature can live out of water.

3 Rewrite the following sentences correcting the errors:
   Neither my brother nor sister were there.
   She missed the train due to her watch being slow.
   They should do it like she does.
   The road is comprised of brick-built bungalows.
   He was the only one who I knew at the dance.
   Jumping on the train his brother greeted her.
   I was sat by the TV when the telephone rang.

Punctuation

1 Using commas or full-stops only, change the punctuation of the following sentences so that each has another meaning. Do not alter the wording in any way.
   No one he knew could mend the broken gear wheel.
   The magistrate said the father was too severe.
   Where do you work in Liverpool?
   The picture was sold for £100 more than it was worth.
   When I arrived at the platform I met Jack and his sister Joan arrived half an hour later.

2 Punctuate the following passage fully:
   if he had taken the trouble to be introduced this wouldnt have happened bertrand said still flushed instead of which he dont worry about it mr dixon the girl cut in it was only a silly misunderstanding

3 Explain the use of the apostrophe and in particular discuss the rule and the usage of the apostrophe to show possession. Give examples.

4 Rewrite the following sentences correctly punctuated, using capital letters where necessary:

His answer was cold i fear my dear charles he said the meaning you attach to scoundrel escapes me

The headmaster addressing the old boys association said there were three things he looked for in his prefects the ability to set a good example absolute honesty and sincerity in all things and loyalty.

5 Rewrite the following passage with correct punctuation and capital letters where necessary:

the adventure required time money and thought it also required many months work johnson hesitated being of a cautious disposition how much do you need he asked oh about £10000 i replied what he exclaimed you cannot mean that besides he added operations are possible only in summer which is too short a period you are on a wild goose chase and i must refuse

Words at work

Put each of the following expressions into a separate sentence which clearly illustrates its meaning:
to make the grade   an anonymous donor
an eccentric person
not responsible for his actions

Interpretation and criticism

Read the following passage carefully, then answer the questions below.

By the time we had finished breakfast, the immense white slopes were infested already with tiny figures, some skimming and criss-crossing like dragon-flies, some faltering and collapsing like injured ants. The skaters were out in dozens on the lake. Knapsacked, helmeted and booted, some of the more active guests were starting out on long, dangerous tours of the upper heights, like soldiers from a luxury barracks. And here and there, amidst the great army, the wounded were to be seen, limping on sticks or with their arms in slings, taking a painful convalescent promenade.
Mr Norris Changes Trains CHRISTOPHER ISHERWOOD
(born 1904)

1 In the first sentence the writer contrasts the size of the slopes with the size of the people on them. Point out the words used to make this contrast.

2 Where do you suppose the more active guests were going?

3 Explain: knapsacked, luxury barracks, convalescent promenade.

4 What is the writer's attitude to this scene?

5 Turn back to the passage on the conquest of Everest on page 96. Then write down four comprehension questions based on the first five paragraphs. Work in pairs and check answers.

Direct and indirect speech

1 Write the following, using the actual words spoken:

The fruit was his, he said, and he would be glad if I would return it at once. He was sure my mother would be very upset and that my father would punish me severely. He asked why I had done it. However, he concluded, he might decide not to tell my parents, if I would apologize immediately.

2 Turn the following reported or indirect speech into direct speech:

He informed the chairman that only that morning he had received an urgent summons which meant that he would have to sail for his homeland the next day. He would always carry with him the liveliest memories of their kindness. If his country were not then on the brink of war, he would have been looking forward to staying among them a little longer in those delightful surroundings.

Reaching a conclusion: changing tastes

Here is a table of figures which appeared in a newspaper (figures are given in millions).

	TEN YEARS AGO	THIS YEAR
1 Books bought	10	75
2 Driving licences issued	$2\frac{1}{2}$	6
3 TV licences issued	2	13
4 Cinema attendances	900	460
5 Football attendances	42	28

Write an account of the conclusions you draw from these figures about the changing leisure habits of the British people. See if there is any connection between the sets of figures – 3 and 4, for example.

See if you can think of reasons for such startling changes as shown in 1. Use your general knowledge to explain the table as fully as you can.

Making a summary

1 Give the following passage a title, and make a summary of it using not more than 40 words:

The canoeing was done on the nearby lake which was five miles long. The canoes were the open type Kayaks and there was also a Red Indian type wooden canoe which was very hard to handle, but supplied us with great amusement whenever anyone tried to use it. At this time of year it was a very cold job, but we went about it in a cheerful manner which is always the case on these Outward Bound courses. When we had got used to canoeing we had an obstacle race which provided us with great fun and laughter.

Everyone who goes on these courses gets something out of it. I did find something in it myself, self-confidence . . .

2 Read the following three paragraphs and then answer the questions which follow.

Complete newspapers, transmitted during the night through existing television sets, may soon be with us. A manager of a large telecommunications firm mentioned that:

'It is technically quite simple now to pass the printed word over the telephonewire that runs to the home without disturbing its normal use. It is certainly a simple matter to use idle time on television channels during the early hours of the morning to transmit a complete newspaper during the hours of sleep.

The main difficulty at the moment in exploiting such ideas is the cost of the receiving printers, but suitable machines could be developed at acceptable cost quite quickly.

Suggest a suitable title for the passage. Set six comprehensive questions on the passage. Write a summary in not more than 30 words.

Figures of speech

1 Give the meaning of these proverbs:
   The pen is mightier than the sword
   Still waters run deep
   Procrastination is the thief of time
   Every cloud has a silver lining
   A new broom sweeps clean
   Empty vessels make most sound

2 Give the meaning of each expression in italics:
   Mr Jones sent us on a *wild-goose chase* and, not
   to beat about the bush, we immediately *smelt a rat*.
   Jack *hit the nail on the head* when he declared that
   his father always had some *bee in his bonnet* and
   he was the sort of person who, if he were *asked*
   to play second fiddle, invariably *got on his high horse*
   and decided to *paddle his own canoe*. A lot of what
   Jack himself said must be *taken with a pinch of*
   salt because he was undoubtedly *a chip off the old*
   block.

Composition or creative writing

1 Make up a short episode which might form part
   of a larger story about a character who is
   waiting to meet someone in one of the following
   situations:
      an airport arrival or departure lounge
      a restaurant
      a coach station
      outside the prison gates
      Bring in as many other characters as you wish.

2 My own view and reasons for and against taking
   a job as ONE of the following:

      a pop singer   a policeman (or policewoman)
      a teacher   a shop assistant
      a factory worker   a farmer

3 Set three suitable composition subjects for your
   group. Now write a composition on one of them.

Test paper

Read the following passage carefully and then
answer the questions which follow.

Most Englishmen are fiercely patriotic, at least
where sport is involved. They follow with
fervour the fluctuating fortunes of their national
representatives in all quarters of the globe, their
attention concentrated on the performance of
teams or individuals as they are reported in the
sports columns of the Press. In this matter of
sport, as in weightier affairs, unity results from
opposition to a common adversary.

But this spirit of concord vanishes the
moment that the strife becomes localised within
this country. National patriotism is whittled
down to the support – difficult to justify – of a
particular team in a country, or a town, or even
a village. Gone is the rare and fascinating
spectacle of the vast majority of Englishmen in
agreement about something.

This local partisanship persists only until
another international match or Test series
comes along: then it is ousted again by complete
but only temporary unity.

1 For each of the following, which are taken from
   the passage, give a word or short phrase which
   could be used to replace it in the passage
   without change of meaning:

involved	fluctuating
concentrated on	whittled down
persists	ousted

2 Explain the meaning of 'local partisanship'.

3 What is meant by describing the adversary as
   'common'?

4 What two different kinds of loyalty does the
   writer suggest? In what circumstances does each
   kind exist?

Appendix one

Other media: useful addresses

Films

Some films have been listed within the particular units with the names and addresses of their distributors. It is also possible to book any film, feature or short through the Central Booking Agency. This is part of the British Film Institute at 81 Dean Street, London WIV 6AA. CBA issue catalogues of the films they possess or can get for you. BFI runs an Information Service which tells you about their films, their distributors, running times, principal actors, etc. – but *not* whether they are available on a particular date.

The Society of Education in Film and Television (SEFT) is also at 81 Dean Street. This organisation publishes a quarterly magazine called *Screen*.

The following addresses are useful for ordering direct from a distributor:

Bargate Films Ltd., National House, 60/66 Wardour Street, London WIV 3HP.
Canada House Film Library, High Commissioner for Canada, Canada House, London SWIY 5BJ.
Columbia Pictures Ltd., Film House, Wardour Street, London, WILV 4AH.
Concord Films Council, Nacton, Ipswich, Suffolk.
Connoisseur Films Ltd., 167 Oxford Street, London WILR 2DX.
Contemporary Films Ltd., 55 Greek Street, London WIV 6DB.

Film Distributors Association (FDA) (16mm) Ltd., P.O. Box 2JL, Mortimer House, 37/41 Mortimer Street, London WIN 7RJ.
Hunter Films Ltd., 182 Wardour Street, London WIV 4BH.
Robert Kingston Films Ltd., 645/7 Uxbridge Road, Hayes End, Middx.
Petroleum Films Bureau, 4 Brook Street, Hanover Square, London WIY 2AY.
National Coal Board, Hobart House, Grosvenor Place, London SWIX 7AE.
Ron Harris Cinema Services Ltd., Glenbuck House, Glenbuck Road, Surbiton, Surrey.
Rank Film Library, PO Box 70, Great West Road, Brentford, Middlesex.
Warner-Pathé Distributors Ltd., Warner-Pathé House, 135 Wardour Street, London WIV 4AP.
Vaughan-Rogosin Films Ltd., 12 Fouberts Place, Regent Street, London WIV 1HH.
Watso Films Ltd., Film House, Charles Street, Coventry.

Gramophone records

Topic Records, 27 Nassington Road,
London NW3 2TX produce a catalogue which lists
records under themes. These are concerned with
folk songs.
e.g. Behan and McColl *Streets of Song* (12T41)
    Louis Killen *Ballads and Broadsides* (12T126)
    Lloyd and McColl *English and Scottish Folk*
                    Ballads (12Y103)
McColl and Seeger *Steam Whistle Ballads* (12T104)
Note: The Philips battery-operated cassette tape-
recorder is ideal for outside recording. The
microphone, however, is very fragile and tends to
go wrong easily.

Sound effects and music

A selection of excellent LP records of sound effects
is available from the BBC.

Out and about

For information, write to the YHA, Trevelyan
House, St. Stephen's Hill, St. Albans, Hertford-
shire. For hostelling abroad write to Y.H.A.
Travel Bureau, 29 John Adam Street, London
WC2N 6JE (and refer to Appendix two on page 131).
Write also for Scottish Sports holidays publication
(free) from Scottish Tourist Board, 2 Rutland
Place, West End, Edinburgh, Scotland.
Consult also The Ramblers' Association about
footpath clearance and the 100 000 miles of public
paths – address: 1–4 Crawford Mews, York Street,
London W1H 1PT. For Orienteering consult British
Orienteering Federation, 3 Glenfinlas Street,
Edinburgh EH3 6YY.

Appendix two

Youth Hostelling abroad: for your information

Your YHA membership card will admit you to Youth Hostels in more than forty different countries throughout the world.

1 **The youth hostels and who may use them**

There are over four thousand youth hostels in the following countries: Argentine, Australia, Austria, Belgium, Bulgaria, Canada, Ceylon, Cyprus, Czechoslovakia, Denmark, Egypt, England and Wales, Finland, France, Germany, Greece, Holland, Hungary, Iceland, India, Ireland, Israel, Italy, Japan, Kenya, Lebanon, Luxembourg, Malaysia, Morocco, New Zealand, Norway, Pakistan, Poland, Portugal, Scotland, South Korea, Spain, Sweden, Switzerland, Syria, Thailand, Tunisia, USA, Yugoslavia.

They offer simple accommodation for walkers and cyclists travelling on their holidays. Each hostel provides a bed, mattress and blankets; separate dormitories for men and for women, with separate washing facilities wherever possible: a kitchen in which visitors can prepare their own meals (note that many German hostels do not provide a kitchen).

Each hostel is supervised by house-parents (or wardens) and at most hostels meals at a reasonable price are provided by the house-parents.

Members are required to take part in the domestic duties of the hostel (cleaning, etc.) as directed by the house-parents. The use of a sheet sleeping-bag of approved pattern is compulsory. Generally, you may not stay more than three consecutive nights at any one youth hostel.

2 **Who may use them?**

In each country there is an independent Youth Hostels Association, which manages its own youth hostels, primarily for the benefit of the young people of its own country. By international agreement, however, a membership card of the Youth Hostels Association (England and Wales), or of the Scottish Youth Hostels Association, is accepted at youth hostels in all other countries, and you do *not* need to become a member of any foreign youth hostels organization.

Note that your YHA membership card must bear your photograph if you wish to use youth hostels outside the British Isles. You attach this yourself, and it does not require stamping.

The normal minimum age for hostelling abroad is 5 years, but it differs in a few countries. There is a maximum age limit of 25 in Switzerland and 27 in Bavaria (South Germany), and in some countries preference is given to younger members.

Continental countries admit users of power-assisted bicycles, motor cycles and motor-cars but priority is always given to walkers and cyclists.

In Scandinavian countries and Israel some youth hostels have rooms set aside for families with young children. Youth hostels are *not* intended as a cheap substitute for hotels; suitcases and smart clothes are out of place, and there is no domestic staff to serve guests. You are advised to get some experience of hostelling in this country before undertaking a trip abroad.

3 **What is the cost?**

The average cost of a youth hostel bed in any country is 40p per night. Meals (where provided) cost from 40p to 50p each. If you buy and cook your own food the cost can be less. In general you should allow at least £1·50 per day to cover bed and three simple meals.

4 **Passports**

To travel abroad you will need either:
(a) A passport, valid for ten years, can be obtained through any Ministry of Labour Employment Exchange, or from the following offices:
   The Passport Office, Clive House, Petty France, London SW1H 9HD.
   Branch Passport Office, Fifth Floor, India Buildings, Water Street, Liverpool 2.
   Branch Passport Office, Westwood, Peterborough.
   Branch Passport Office, Olympia House, Dock Street, Newport, Mon.
   Branch Passport Office, 131 West Nile Street, Glasgow C1, or
(b) For travelling to Western Europe you can obtain a British Visitor's Passport, valid for twelve months, from your nearest Ministry of Labour Employment Exchange. Enquire also at your Post Office. It cannot be obtained from the Passport Offices and it cannot be used for Yugoslavia or East European countries.

5 **Travel to and from Europe**

The main expense of a Continental holiday is the fare from Britain. In summer there are cheap night returns from London to the Belgian and French ports and beyond. Full tables of fares, routes, etc., are given in the *YHA Continental Travel Key.*

6 **Taking money abroad**

You should purchase travellers' cheques and some foreign money before you go abroad. This can be done through YHA Travel or any bank whether you hold an account or not.

British residents are allowed foreign exchange facilities up to the equivalent of £300 per person for each journey abroad, and such transactions have to be entered in your passport. In addition to foreign currency and travellers' cheques you may take up to £25 in sterling notes with you each time you leave the United Kingdom.

7 **Where are the hostels?**

Each association publishes a handbook giving the addresses and full details of its hostels. This information is in the language of the country concerned but usually there is an explanation in English, or the IYHF sign language is used. The handbooks are on sale from YHA Services, 29 John Adam Street, London WC2N 6JE, and new editions become available mostly between April and June each year. Before this date the previous year's editions can sometimes be purchased. Alternatively, the International Handbook contains addresses and brief details of all the permanent hostels in Europe.

8 **Booking accommodation in advance**

It is advisable to book accommodation in advance at hostels abroad during July and August and at youth hostels in major cities at any time of the year. To make reservation you should use the special advance booking postcards published by YHA Services, which are printed in six languages. They can be used to include several people, and requests for meals can be made on them. Each card should be posted in an envelope, together with an International Reply Coupon (on sale at Post Offices), direct to the hostels. Note that you are not asked to prepay your bookings. Cancellations must be notified to the wardens as soon as possible. There is no special cancellation card, but a note of suitable phrases is included in the *YHA Continental Travel Key*. Generally there is no set limit to the time ahead that you can book, but three months is considered sufficient.

9 Maps

Most of the foreign youth hostel handbooks contain a small scale map showing the general location of the hostels and this will help you to plan your holiday. For your actual walking or cycling trip, however, you will require more detailed maps; a wide range of foreign maps is available from YHA Services Ltd.

10 Routes

Members can plan their own routes by making use of the *Youth Hosteller's Guide to Europe* and the *International Youth Hostel Handbook*. The following should be borne in mind:

Youth hostels are too scattered to allow hostel-to-hostel walking tours in the mountain areas, except in Germany and parts of Scandinavia, Vosges and Swiss Alps. In the Alps there are many mountain huts at high altitudes, run on similar lines to youth hostels, but in no way connected with them. In many parts of France and most of Spain and south Italy hostels are too far apart for one day's cycling. The Ile de France and the coast of Normandy and Brittany are fairly well served, but it is difficult to get inexpensive accommodation in Paris. Outside the main summer season most hostels in Denmark, Finland, Norway, Sweden, Poland and Spain are closed. The only itineraries prepared by the Association for individual members are those mentioned in the paragraph headed Independent Holidays.

11 Insurance

There is no National Health Service on the Continent (except in Denmark, Norway, Sweden and Yugoslavia) and hospital fees, etc., are very heavy indeed. Intending travellers are strongly advised to insure against medical expenses, personal accident, loss of personal effects, etc. Details will be supplied by YHA Travel.

12 Parties

Many Continental hostels are too small to accept school parties or other large groups. The most suitable countries for party tours are Holland, Luxembourg, Switzerland, Denmark and Western Germany. Parties of ten or more can obtain reduced fares through YHA Travel.

YHA travel services

ENQUIRIES: Enquiries from YHA members, personal and postal, are answered without charge – a postage stamp for reply should accompany postal enquiries – but members are asked to make sure that their question is not already answered in the national or international handbooks or the publications listed on page 134.

HANDBOOKS, MAPS, EQUIPMENT Full details of the service offered by YHA Services will be found in the following publications, available from 29 John Adam Street, London, WC2N 6JE. *Maps, handbooks, guides.* A leaflet containing details of the foreign handbooks that are available and a comprehensive list of British and foreign maps together with a selection of phrase books and travel guides.
Equipment for hostellers and campers. A fully illustrated catalogue of equipment for the hosteller and camper.
Equipment for climbers and cavers. A brochure illustrating equipment for the climber and caver.

Equipment for skiers. Published each year in October; a brochure describing and illustrating a range of inexpensive and attractive ski wear and equipment. *Books of interest to hostellers*. A selective list from our very wide range of countryside and travel books.

RAIL, BOAT AND AIR TICKETS As accredited agents for British Railways and all the Continental railway and steamship companies, YHA Travel can supply travel tickets to all destinations and secure seat, couchette and sleeper reservations. Air travel can also be booked through YHA Travel.

REDUCED FARES The YHA can offer concessional fares on the ferry services to Holland, party-travel fares mentioned in the paragraph headed Independent Holidays and attractive YHA Rail Tours as indicated in the next paragraph. Apart from these, there are no reduced rate tickets for members travelling independently for holiday purposes.

Ask for leaflet TRAV/11 dealing with shipping and ferry services between Britain and Continental ports, or for TRAV/4 covering bookings for international railway journeys.

Some European countries offer travel concessions to full-time students attending summer schools or courses at their universities. Details can be had from YHA Travel or, in the case of cheap charter flights, from NUS Travel, 117 Euston Road, London NW1 2SX.

EUROPEAN RAIL TOURS You can travel to a European destination and back with a YHA summer tour party, making a considerable saving on fares, and have hostels booked for you, keeping to one of the suggested itineraries or making your own choice of route.

Ask for details of these Continental holidays described in the brochure TRAV/13.

INDEPENDENT HOLIDAYS YHA Travel have also arranged independent holidays to Belgium, Luxembourg and Holland and to Scandinavia at very attractive rates. Ask for leaflet TRAV/13A.

SCHOOL AND YOUTH GROUP HOLIDAYS The YHA are specialists in low-priced British and Continental holidays for school and youth groups. Booklet TRAV/19 has details of over eighty summer and winter sports holidays arranged for young people at especially low prices ranging from seven days in England to thirteen days in Italy visiting Venice, Florence, Sorrento and Rome.

Three books you need for planning your hostel tour abroad

The International Youth Hostel Handbook, Volume I. Contains addresses and brief details of all the permanent hostels in Europe, North Africa and the Near East (approximately 2 200), together with the principal hostel regulations for all countries. Text in English, French and German. Incorporates a large folding map of Europe showing the location of all hostels. 160 pages, with coloured cover. Available in March each year. Volume II of the *International Youth Hostel Handbook* contains details of hostels in Australasia, America and Asia.
Youth Hosteller's Guide Books, e.g., *Youth Hosteller's Guide to Europe* are mines of information. They are guides to the principal routes and touring areas, how to see them economically and what to see, with background information about the peoples and their ways of life. They include:
Benelux, Denmark/Iceland, France, Germany, Greece/Yugoslavia, Italy, Austria, Norway, Spain/Portugal, Sweden/Finland, Switzerland, Britain.
Youth Hosteller's Guide to Europe is the complete edition of all the chapters listed above. New edition, 492 pages, 31 maps, 33 street plans, revised and reset, bound in stiff boards.
The YHA Continental Travel Key. Practical current information to supplement the *Youth Hosteller's Guide to Europe*; passport and money regulations, rail and boat fares and time-tables.
Consult YHA Travel, 29 John Adam Street, London WC2N 6JE. Telephone: 01–839 1722 also at 36/38 Fountain Street, Manchester M2 2BE and 35 Cannon Street, Birmingham B2 5EE.

Index

Acknowledgements

We are grateful to the following for permission to reproduce copyright material:
The Bodley Head for 'Val's Perfect Crime' by E Stucley from *Magnolia Buildings*; The British Broadcasting Corporation for an extract from 'The Conquest of Everest' which was included in their pamphlet, *Exploration and Discovery*, Autumn 1972; Curtis Brown Ltd for an extract from the poem, 'All-In Wrestlers' by James Kirkup; Consumers' Association for 'What makes a good shoe?' from *Which?* September 1973; J M Dent & Sons Ltd and the Trustees for the copyrights of the late Dylan Thomas, for an extract from *Under Milkwood* by Dylan Thomas and an extract from *Quite Early One Morning* by Dylan Thomas; Faber & Faber Ltd for 'The Storm' from *The Collected Poems of Theodore Roethke* by Theodore Roethke; Leslie Frewin Publishers Ltd for 'The Sportsman' from *Dorset Village* by Clive Sansom; author for an extract from *Pie in the Sky* by Tony Gibson; Victor Gollanz Ltd for 'Superman' from *Hoping for a Hoopoe* by John Updike; Harcourt Brace Jovanovich Inc., for 'Jazz Fantasia' from *Smoke and Steel* by Carl Sandburg, copyright, 1920, by Harcourt Brace Jovanovich, Inc, copyright, 1948 by Carl Sandburg, and 'Aw nuts aw go peddle yer papers' from *The People, Yes* by Carl Sandburg, copyright 1936, by Harcourt Brace Jovanovich, Inc, renewed, 1964 by Carl Sandburg. Reprinted by permission of the publishers; The Executors of the Hemingway Estate and Jonathan Cape Ltd for an extract from 'The Old Man at the Bridge' by Ernest Hemingway from *The First Forty-Nine Stories*; The Trustees of the Hardy Estate, The Macmillan Company of Canada and Macmillan, London and Basingstoke for 'Throwing a Tree: New Forest' and 'At the Railway Station, Upway' from *Collected Poems* by Thomas Hardy; authors' agent for an extract from *The Kraken Wakes* by John Wyndham, published by Michael Joseph Ltd; Hodder and Stoughton Ltd for an extract from *Space Below My Feet* by Gwen Moffat; the author for his article, 'Wembley Story: The White Horse' by Frank Keating which appeared in *The Guardian*, 5.5.73; The Labour Party for the article 'Toe Deformities from Consumer Action' by Mary McCurrie from *Labour Weekly*, 2.2.73; Longman Group Ltd for an extract from *The English Imagination* by Stuart Holroyd; McGraw-Hill Ryerson Ltd for the poem 'The Twenty-Fifth of December' from *The Colour of the Times/Ten Elephants On Yonge Street* by Raymond Souster. Reprinted by permission of the publisher, McGraw-Hill Ryerson Limited; John Murray (Publishers) Ltd for 'Harvest Hymn' from *Collected Poems* by John Betjeman; Penguin Books Ltd for 'Lies' and 'The Companion' from *Selected Poems* by Yevgeny Yevtushenko translated by Robin Milner-Gulland and Peter Levi, S J (Penguin Modern European Poets 1962) © Robin Milner-Gulland and Peter Levi, 1962; Jonathan Cape Ltd for 'Headline History' from *Collected Poems* by William Plomer; Laurence Pollinger Ltd and the Estate of the late Mrs Frieda Lawrence for an extract from 'Odour of Chrysanthemums' by D H Lawrence from *The Complete Short Stories of D H Lawrence*; the author for his article 'Olympic Games' by John Rodda which appeared in *The Guardian*, 5.5.73; Marie Rodell, Literary Trustee and Hamish Hamilton Ltd for an extract from *Silent Spring* by Rachel Carson; Routledge & Kegan Paul Ltd for the poem 'The Lorry Driver' by Peter Halliwell; Charles Scribner's Sons for 'Water Picture' by May Swenson from *To Mix With Time* reprinted by permission of Charles Scribner's Sons. Copyright © 1963 May Swenson; Sidgwick & Jackson Ltd for the poem 'The Bridge' by J Redwood Anderson;

the author for the poem 'Climbing' from *Windy Boy in a Windswept Tree* by Prof. Geoffrey Summerfield; Times Newspaper Limited for the article, 'Trials of a dog who has to work for his living' by Edward Hart from *The Times*, 10.2.73 and an article from the *Sunday Times Colour Supplement*, March 1973. © The Sunday Times; Trans World Feature Syndicate Inc, for the articles, 'For your information: London's other underground line' and 'Safety Code for holiday climbers', and Syndication International for the feature 'You Can't help yourself, can you Madam?' by Alex Valentine from the *Mirror Colour Magazine* 6th December, 1969.

We have been unable to trace the following copyright holders and would appreciate receiving any information that would enable us to do so: J M Harwood, for 'Some are Born Great' (with apologies to Ian Fleming) and Martin Page for the article 'Night Riders' which appeared in *The Guardian*, 11.3.61, and B S Johnson for the poem 'Song of the Wagondriver' which appeared in the BBC pamphlet *Living Language*.

We are grateful to the following for permission to reproduce photographs:
Barnaby's Picture Library, page 99 (top); Camera Press, page 37 (left); Culver Pictures, page 38; Department of the Environment, page 4; Donaldson and Sons, page 22; Mary Evans Picture Library, page 28 (top left), 28 (top right), 28 (bottom left and right), 36 (right); Graphische Sammlung, Vienna, page 66 (right); The Guardian, page 43; Guildhall Art Gallery, page 77 (top); Nicholas Hall, page 5 (top); John Hillelson Agency Ltd, page 35 (left) and 82; London Express News and Feature Service, page 78 (top); Mansell Collection pages 13 (above left), 14 (top left) and 37 (top right); Museum of Modern Art, page 66; Master and Fellows of Magdalene College, Cambridge, pages 77 and 78; Mirror Colour supplement, page 21; New York Daily News Photos, pages 37 (bottom right) and 91 (right); P & A Photos, page 7; David Perlmutter, page 94; Philips Electrical Ltd, page 56; Picturepoint, pages 2, 45, 46 (Photo Francis Browne), 57 and 105; Radio Times Hulton Picture Library, pages 13 (top right), 14 (bottom left), 39, 99 (bottom) and 113; Sport and General Press Agency, page 41; Stedelijk Museum, Amsterdam, page 102 (bottom); A W Swallow, Chelsea School of Chiropody, page 30 (top, centre and bottom); Syndication International, pages 5 (bottom right), 6 and 111; Tate Gallery, pages 61 and 119; The Times, pages 36 (left); Transport and Road Research Laboratory, Department of the Environment, page 80; Transworld Feature Syndication, pages 33, 34 and 35 (right).

We are also grateful to the following for permission to reproduce artwork:
1800 Woodcuts by Thomas Bewick and His School, Dover Publications, pages 103 and 104; BMRB Cooking Attitudes 1961, page 32; British Broadcasting Corporation Autumn 1972, Exploration and Discovery, pages 97 and 98; British Rail, page 79; British Caledonian Airways, pages 95 and 96; Her Majesty's Stationery Office, page 81; Charles Keeping and BBC, Living Language Pamphlet Autumn 1972, pages 101/2.